Call me evil, let me go

Call me evil, let me go

A mother's struggle to save her children
from a brutal religious cult

SARAH JONES

HarperElement
An Imprint of HarperCollins*Publishers*
77–85 Fulham Palace Road,
Hammersmith, London W6 8JB

www.harpercollins.co.uk

and *HarperElement* are trademarks of
HarperCollins*Publishers* Ltd

First published by HarperElement 2011

1 3 5 7 9 10 8 6 4 2

© Sarah Jones 2011

Sarah Jones asserts the moral right to be
identified as the author of this work

A catalogue record of this book
is available from the British Library

ISBN 978-0-00-743356-8

Printed and bound in Great Britain by
Clays Ltd, St Ives plc

Mixed Sources
Product group from well-managed
forests and other controlled sources
www.fsc.org Cert no. SW-COC-001806
© 1996 Forest Stewardship Council

FSC is a non-profit international organisation established to promote the
responsible management of the world's forests. Products carrying the FSC
label are independently certified to assure consumers that they come
from forests that are managed to meet the social, economic and
ecological needs of present and future generations.

Find out more about HarperCollins and the environment at
www.harpercollins.co.uk/green

To all my beautiful children and to all the broken lives that cults have left in their wake

Chapter 1

Shocking Revelations

The phone rang just as I started cooking spaghetti bolognese for the children's tea. It was the junior-school head. Even though she knew me well her voice sounded harsh, cold, and formal and my heart immediately started pounding. I could sense that I was in for a telling-off. Again. Without any preamble she said that my son Paul had been very naughty at school that afternoon. He had been messing around with some other boys after football, throwing the caked mud that had collected on their boots everywhere and, worst of all, he had even thrown a piece into another boy's face, cutting him slightly and making him cry. She told me I had to 'deal with him' at home.

I thought her formality was a bit over the top and asked if there had been any teachers in the changing room while this was going on. She admitted there hadn't been, and I thought to myself that it wasn't too much to worry about and that boys will be boys. Even so, I was gripped with tension. I knew only too well that being told to 'deal with him' was an unspoken order to smack Paul. He, along with his sister Rebecca and his brothers Luke and Daniel, went to Tadford School, a small establishment that belonged to Tadford Charismatic Church in the south of England.

The Charismatic movement is not a church in itself, but includes many different churches. Its members believe that faith must be deeply felt rather than just experienced through ritual. Tadford was under the overall control of its founder and pastor, Ian Black, and was unlike any other church. He was a controversial, powerful, supremely confident man who regularly preached that it was important to break a child's will early and believed in corporal punishment.

I had grown used to being told what to do by the Church leaders, and especially Ian Black, ever since my parents had placed me in their care years earlier, when I was in my mid-teens. I'd been desperate not to be uprooted from my family home in a small market town in the Pennines, to board at Tadford, as it was far too far away from family and friends, but my well-meaning parents, particularly my mother Pamela, were worried that what they saw as my increasingly rebellious teenage behaviour meant I was on a slippery downward path.

They believed that a school with strict religious guide-lines, firm discipline and an inflexible routine would do me good.

Although my feisty spirit had largely been squashed over the years, it had never quite been extinguished and I had a reputation for not always toeing the line. But the phone call on that cold November evening shook me to the core and I was anxious to get away. 'OK, I'll deal with it', I said, then put down the phone.

I knew the head was right, in that Paul had been naughty, but I thought it was just the sort of silly thing a boy of his age might do, especially when no teacher was present. I also wondered why I hadn't been told about it when I collected Paul from school. I glanced at my watch. It was just after 5 p.m. I knew I had better sort Paul out before my husband Peter came home from work as he was likely to be far tougher on Paul than I would be.

I called Paul. 'Will you come into Mummy and Daddy's bedroom, please,' I said, trying not to let my anxiety show in my voice. 'I want to speak to you.' I didn't want to punish him in front of his siblings.

Paul was struggling with his homework in the bedroom he had to share with Rebecca. He had dysgraphia, a writing disorder, and the help the school had given him had, six months earlier, suddenly been withdrawn without warning or explanation, and as a result he was finding schoolwork much harder.

I told him about the phone call, and he admitted that he, along with some of his friends, had been silly. It wasn't, he insisted, just his fault. I listened carefully to his explanation and told him he had been naughty. I then pulled down his trousers and underpants and gave him two quick smacks with my hand on his bare bottom. After that I cuddled him tightly, pleased that he didn't cry. I hated smacking him, but I knew that if I didn't Peter would and it would be far worse.

As all four children ate their supper Paul didn't seem at all concerned about being smacked. No more was said until a couple of hours later when Peter arrived home from a nearby town, where he was working as a fitness coach. Peter and I were not getting on well. We had married when I was only 18 and very naive. He was several years older than me and, if possible, even more innocent, but the Church encouraged its young members to marry early, so we did what was expected of us. I always felt suspicious that ours was an arranged match, but I had genuinely come to love Peter. I also knew I was lucky to have a husband at all, because you could only marry within the Church and there weren't always enough young men to go round.

Sadly our marriage had recently become little more than an empty shell. Peter seemed to be permanently in a bad temper and was hardly at home, choosing instead to spend any spare time – when he wasn't working late at the fitness centre – helping out in the Church. Soon after he got back from work I told him what had happened at school, and made a point of adding that I had dealt with Paul and smacked him. Peter ignored my comments, went straight to find Paul and took him into our bedroom, grabbing as he did so a squash racquet that was lying by the door. He then smacked Paul's bare bottom several times with it.

I was mortified. Paul was our first child, but still our baby. He needed our protection, not our anger. When it was over he went straight back to the bedroom he shared with Rebecca without saying a word. He stayed there for the rest of the evening, and wouldn't speak to me when I tucked him up for the night. Paul and I had always been close and his silence was like a dagger in my heart. He might have been brave enough not to cry, but I wasn't. I wept for him. I thought it was totally wrong to hit him like that, and couldn't bear the thought of his pain, but I knew from experience it was pointless to say anything to Peter, let alone criticize him. If I protested he was likely to fly into a rage. But I hated myself for being so weak.

I knew if I confronted Peter he'd also tell Ian Black, who ran the Church with a rod of iron, what had happened, and he would certainly haul me into his grand office and go through his usual emotional battering. This included telling me in very strong language

5

that I was rebellious, or worse. Although he was a religious leader he didn't mind his language, and it seemed to me that he enjoyed trying to undermine me.

Paul was still very subdued the next day, a Friday, but went to school without any fuss. When I collected him in the afternoon he told me, with no apparent emotion, that he had been 'whacked' – beaten with a shoe that was kept in the classroom and used to hit children if they disobeyed one of the school's many rules. I was furious that he had been beaten without my knowledge or agreement. It meant that my poor little boy had been punished not once, not twice, but three times for the same, not very serious, offence.

I was cross that none of the teachers told me what had happened when I was picking Paul up, but shortly after we got home, the phone rang. It was Patricia, one of his teachers, who told me officially that he had been smacked. I was so angry I gave her short shrift. I said that I had been specifically told by the head to deal with Paul's punishment at home and that, contrary to what was the school's normal procedure, I hadn't been told in advance that he would be hit, nor had I given anyone permission to do so. She didn't say much and the conversation was quickly over.

I felt desperately sorry for Paul. He seemed withdrawn and uncommunicative, so I gave him lots of extra attention. When Peter came home that evening I told him how annoyed I was that the school had disciplined him after clearly saying they would leave it to me. He barely reacted. His uncle and aunt, who had brought him up after his parents had been killed in a boating accident, were founder members of the Church and he believed that anything the Church did was automatically right whereas any opinion I voiced against it was automatically wrong.

Paul went to school as usual on Saturday. He had lessons in the morning, played football in the afternoon, then had a violin lesson and choir practice. On Sunday morning and evening he came with the rest of the family to church. It was an utterly miserable weekend. Paul barely spoke a word the whole time. I felt totally distraught that I had let him down. He had been treated so appallingly that I wanted to take him out of the school immediately. But realistically I knew it wasn't an option. It was compulsory for all members of the Church to send their children to the Church school. Any other course of action was unthinkable.

But as the days passed, Paul's unfairly harsh punishment weighed increasingly heavily on me and I began to feel that the Church had taken away not just my control over my child but also my parental rights. In addition, I slowly started to realize that it wasn't just my children they were in control of, but that my own mind, body and emotions were being run by the Church.

I'd never thought about it with such clarity before, but the incident prompted me to wonder how I had accepted as inevitable something as wrong as hitting children. It made me feel terrible. I was very maternal and adored my children, yet I was unable to protect them or even have the support of their father. I was desperate to talk my anxieties through with someone, but didn't know where to turn. My life, like those of nearly all the Church members, was centred entirely on Tadford Charismatic Church. I was cut off from my family and former friends and had nowhere to go to express my concern or get help.

Tadford actively discouraged members from associating with anyone who wasn't part of the community. We were repeatedly told that the world outside the Church was a horrendous place and that there were no true Christians except those who came to Tadford, not even Christians who attended other churches. On the rare occasions the idea of leaving the Church fleetingly crossed my mind, I was instantly enveloped by a paralysing fear and put it right out of my thoughts. Over the years, Black had given his congregation many examples of individuals who had left the Church subsequently being struck down by God and I believed to my core that if I left I too would die. So although it was now clear to me that something was wrong with a Church that believed in corporal punishment, I couldn't take it any further. Instead I tried to immerse myself in making improvements to our new house. I loved creating a nest for my family and, although it didn't change anything fundamentally, it worked on one level as a diversion.

Several weeks passed and one Tuesday afternoon I decided to go into a nearby town to buy some curtain material for the twins' new bedroom. It was market day and I took along my friend Megan, another Church member, who was older than me and had kindly offered to make the curtains. I bought some fabric with thin blue, red and white stripes for the twins' room and another with a design of leaping dolphins for the bath-room. Neither was expensive and I came home feeling very pleased.

The following day I was called into Black's office. This usually meant trouble and I assumed it was some-thing to do with my work. All adult Church members had to put in many hours of 'voluntary' work for the Church. I'd had various jobs and was now recording and editing the pastor's sermons and his regular sessions of what he called 'miracle healing'.

I worked while the children were at school, in the evenings after they went to bed, at weekends and when the Church arranged conferences. Not surprisingly, I felt permanently exhausted. As soon as I arrived at Black's office he told me off about a faulty recording I had produced. Then, to my astonishment, he turned his attention to my recent shopping trip. Although all my four children were of school age, he asked how dare I go off without permission, leaving 'others' to look after them. I explained I went to get curtain material for our new home, but he repeated that I had no right to do so without asking first. It was absurd. I had gone in my free time, while the children were at the school, for which we paid fees, and the 'others' he referred to were in fact their teachers.

I was often intimidated by Black, but on this occasion I said to myself, 'This is ridiculous. I'm a grown woman and I'm still being treated like the teenage girl I was when I first arrived. I can't carry on like this.' Later I found out that Megan didn't get into trouble for coming with me.

The trouble was, I couldn't think of a concrete plan to change my situation. I consoled myself with the thought that, largely thanks to my job recording Black's sermons, at least my eyes were open now in that I was more aware of how the Church operated. His 'miracle healing' events regularly took place on a Sunday, when individuals of different ages who were suffering from a range of illnesses, including arthritis and cancer, would come to the Church in the desperate hope that they would be healed. The routine was that, at various points in the two-hour assembly, Black would choose a few of these invalids to talk to. He would use a hand-held microphone to record what he was saying, then ask what was wrong with them. Regardless of the malady, he would tell them almost immediately that they had been cured.

If, for example, they had a problem walking he would firmly take their hand, pull them from their seat, and then half drag them forward and back in front of the congregation at an ever-faster pace until they were almost running, claiming loudly throughout that Jesus had cured them. The mood of these meetings was highly charged and intensely emotional, and the sick, their loved ones and many members of the congregation would almost always weep.

I noticed that Black was careful not to claim that he did the healing himself, but the way he spoke and behaved made it easy to assume that Jesus was using him as the conduit for the 'miracle' to take place.

It was my job to record these traumatic sessions, edit them and add any necessary sound effects, and produce a half-hour CD that the Church could sell to the general public. To make sure I encapsulated the essence of the occasion, I had to spend a lot of time studying how Black worked and what he said. As a result I became acutely aware of his techniques and choice of language. His voice was constantly on my computer's speakers (I did my editing with some software I had bought) and, almost imperceptibly, he gradually lost his hold on me.

As he did so I began increasingly to think for myself. This isn't as easy as it sounds because for so many years I believed Jesus used Black to talk to us and express His wishes. I felt that God Himself was eternally grateful that Black was alive. This gave Black massive power and inhibited a very ordinary person like me from questioning such a man about any area of his life.

Once I developed some distance I watched and listened to him more objectively and became increasingly cynical about his 'miracle cures', particularly as I would also often have to interview these sick people after their sessions with him to get some words of testimony from them. This meant I saw for myself that his claims that they were cured weren't true. Although some managed to walk or run with Black in the heat of the moment, their problems always returned a couple of days later.

Because I had to edit Black's sermons I became very familiar with his expressions and speech patterns. I listened as he ruthlessly criticized people who weren't in the Church, dismissed those who were getting old, peppered some sermons with sexual innuendo and regularly made serious allegations, often of a sexual nature, about individuals, most of which I didn't believe at all. My job was to make the sermons respectable for public consumption. I made sure I deleted his sexual innuendo and slanderous comments. Ironically, spending my formative years in a strict cult had left its moral mark and I didn't think it was right for any Christian to talk in such a negative way about any individual and it was certainly not how a religious leader should think, let alone behave.

The finished CDs were meant to enhance Black's reputation and bring in new members. They were also a useful source of income as they were sold in the Church shop or sent out via mail order from the Church catalogue. Bit by bit, my resentment spread to other areas of my life and once I began to question Black's behaviour I started to resent and reject the Church's overall control of what I did, said and felt. For example, I couldn't watch TV soaps because Black described them as evil. Nor was I allowed to listen to secular music, either modern or classical, as Black said it contained evil spirits. The exception was the music of Bach, whom Black described as being a true Christian. Instead, Church members were encouraged to spend their spare time listening to CDs of him preaching.

Peter and I even had to ask permission to go on holiday. Not that we went very often. We were too busy working for the Church, and besides had no spare money. Like all members, we were expected to hand over tithes, which were at least a tenth of our gross salary, to the Church, give additional amounts for 'special occasions' and pay hefty school fees. I couldn't even freely choose what I or my children wore. Respectable women of the Church weren't allowed to wear trousers, a skirt above the knee, or show even a hint of cleavage, and the children had to be dressed in tweeds and blazers like little adults.

My birthday was approaching and, as happened every year near that time, it was an opportunity to take stock. I felt that in many ways I had grown and matured, but in others I was still being treated like a child. It annoyed me. I didn't want to be told what I could and couldn't do and how I should think any more, but working out how to change this was too big a reality for me to contemplate. I just knew I couldn't carry on in the same way. The main problem was that I had so little experience of making decisions. Most people learn about decision-making gradually as they grow up. But I had been emotionally pummelled into obedience during my most formative years by Black and other senior members of the Church. I had almost no control over my life or my children.

Not that I dared mention what I felt to a soul. I couldn't confide in Peter, who, when he wasn't working long hours at his day job, spent his time at the Church, or in a single friend, as anything I said would have gone straight back to Black, and I was terrified of him and the power he had over me. I badly needed to explore my fledgling thoughts. I wanted to find out if anyone else felt the same as I did and, like me, longed to be comforted or reassured. Instead I bottled up everything deep inside me, kept my inner turmoil completely hidden and somehow dealt with it all myself. It was particularly difficult as I'm naturally gregarious, but for the moment to behave differently seemed as difficult as swimming against a tidal wave. Even if you slightly criticized either an ordinary member of the Church or one of the elders, everyone got to hear about it and you could be ostracized. The prospect was too awful to contemplate and I likened it to solitary confinement. I couldn't risk that as my whole life revolved around the Church. I had barely seen my parents or my sister during my years away and didn't feel close to them. I had no other adult contacts outside – everything of my pre-Church life had been severed. I had nowhere to go. Nor, I realized when I thought pragmatically about my situation, did I have any money of my own.

It was a huge struggle but I managed to keep my thoughts to myself until one day, about five months after Paul had been beaten, I was on my way to the recording room after I'd taken the children to school, when I bumped into another Church member, Susan. We started talking and she daringly grumbled that she wasn't allowed to go on a holiday when she wanted to. 'It's ridiculous,' she said. 'This place is just like a bloody cult.'

I had never heard the Church described like that, and it had never crossed my mind in all the years I had been at Tadford that what I was trapped in, and controlled by, had the characteristics of a cult. I wasn't even absolutely sure what a cult was. I didn't say anything to Susan, because my head went into a complete spin and alarm bells began to ring so loudly in my ears I felt I would explode.

When I calmed down a little I remembered that there was a Christian bookshop in town that we weren't allowed to go to. Black had told us it was evil because it was run by Christians who weren't members of Tadford. Perhaps, I thought, the answers to the thousand of questions that were flooding my brain could be there. I rushed into the recording room, which was in a small room in the church.

My friend Kath, who had been at Tadford for just over a year, was helping out that day and was already hard at work editing the recording of the recent spring conference. Instead of saying 'Hello', I almost barked at her, 'Pack up. We're going out.' We locked the room and when I whispered our destination in her ear her eyes opened wide, but she saw how intense I was and didn't say a word.

Bearing in mind that we weren't allowed to go out without permission and I had no idea if Kath would be on my side, I was taking a big risk. I certainly hadn't thought it through. It was as if something more powerful than myself was pushing me forward. Part of me was in a complete panic, but there was also a quiet but firm voice in my brain telling me that Kath always seemed to keep her own counsel and I should trust my instinct. We got into my car and I drove into the centre of town as if my life depended on it, which indeed I felt it did. I was convinced that at any second God would strike me dead because I wasn't doing His will. There could be no greater sin than deliberately disobeying orders and going to a bookshop run by people who would surely go to Hell. Sooner or later that would be my destination too, I thought, even if I were lucky enough to be spared for the next half-hour. My dicing with fate seemed more dangerous than leaping off Mount Everest blindfolded on a dark, freezing night. Utter madness. My choice of destination would also inevitably mean I would lose my children to the secular world – something I'd repeatedly been told was a fate worse than death. It didn't occur to me to question what type of God could be so capricious as to strike you down for going to a bookshop without permission.

I was shaking like a leaf by the time I arrived in town and parked by the bookshop. I looked around, half expecting to see a celestial firing squad lined up on the pavement waiting for me. There was nothing. I was equally relieved to see no one I knew nearby. As we walked into the bookshop I took a deep breath. My heart was beating incredibly fast. I wanted to get out as soon as possible and try to save my life. I looked desperately along the shelves, at first too scared to focus or read any of the titles. Then suddenly my eyes lighted on a slim white book entitled *When a Church Becomes a Cult*, by Stephen Wookey. I looked quickly around for Kath, pulled her over, pointed at the book and with shaking hands took two copies off the shelves. I gave her one and we each paid for our own copy. Then I drove back to Tadford as fast as I could, feeling a strange mixture of terror and exhilaration as I quickly prayed for my life to be spared.

I dared not go home in case someone spotted me, reported me to Black and I was hauled into his office and asked why I wasn't working. So I suggested to Kath that we go back to the recording room. She agreed and as soon as we were safely inside we locked the door. It was something I did when I had a lot to do and didn't want to be disturbed, so in itself that wouldn't arouse suspicion. If someone should knock on the door and want to speak to either of us for whatever reason, I decided, I would sit on the book. Kath and I then sat at adjacent desks and began reading our books. I took a green highlighter and marked the sentences that meant something to me. There were so many I nearly ran out of ink. I also began crying so much I could hardly breathe. I have never read anything so fast, but it was vital to dash through it before anyone disturbed us. At the same time I couldn't skip a single word. The contents mesmerized me and I recognized an enormous amount of similarity between what was being described in the book and my life at Tadford. As I turned each page I realized more and more clearly what sort of place I was in. It felt as if I were being given a powerful electric shock that was reawakening the real me that had been crushed for so many years. My reaction was that every-thing about my life at Tadford was completely shattered and that I had been part of one big lie. I saw with rare clarity that I had to get out. The only question was: how?

Chapter 2

My Family and I

I was born Sarah Alice Weston, the third child and second daughter of Pamela and John Weston. My father worked as an electrician in the Merchant Navy, my mother was a florist. Home was a spacious three-storey, semi-detached, five-bedroom house with a large garden in a market town in the Pennines.

Apart from me, my family consisted of Kerry, who was 11 when I was born, and Roy, 12. My sister was easy-going and well behaved, but there was something not quite right about my brother. I couldn't have known then that he was to affect my life profoundly.

Roy was by all accounts an adorable baby and grew into a bright, intelligent little boy much praised for his all-round ability by his teachers at his local school. My doting parents took great pride in his success, and not too much notice when his teachers added that he was a bit of a loner and didn't mix well. He was, after all, the first child in our family and Mum didn't know what to expect. She assumed he was taking after her and she was not one to go out with a crowd of girls. She didn't even worry that he kept himself to himself at home too, putting it down to the fact that he was behaving like any boy with two younger sisters.

Certainly Roy didn't take much notice of me when I arrived, but Kerry was delighted to have a little sister. Roy's life and that of my family changed dramatically almost overnight one day when I was just a sweet, bubbly toddler. Many parents worry about their child turning into Kevin, the iconic teenager created by comedian Harry Enfield, when they reach their teens, but Roy's transformation was far more extreme. He stopped being the loving lad who was good at so many things, and turned into an impossible rebel with an explosive temper who screamed and shouted at the least thing.

He used to be immaculate and tidy, but became extremely scruffy and left his bedroom in a terrible mess. Worst of all he no longer wanted to go to school and began playing truant. It was shortly after his birthday that we had the first clear sign that something was seriously wrong. He was playing rock music so loudly in his bedroom that the house started to reverberate. Dad went in and asked him to turn the volume down. To his horror, instead of replying Roy jumped up and down on his bed with his fingers in his ears, screaming. Now, when most children of that age start screaming in a tantrum they stop pretty quickly afterwards, but Roy scream lasted for over ten minutes. It was then that my parents knew for certain that their son's behaviour had gone beyond that of even the most difficult teenager.

Mental health was very poorly handled in the sixties and seventies, with little diagnosis and even less support. When my parents took Roy to see our trusted family GP they believed everything he said implicitly and didn't query his diagnosis that Roy was just a typical adolescent. He said that, of course, it was unusual behaviour, but 'these things happen and they shouldn't worry'. They did worry, of course, and felt very guilty about his obvious unhappiness, racking their brains to remember something they might have done that triggered this change in him. But they couldn't come up with anything.

Roy was particularly awful when my widowed maternal grandma came to live with us that year. He started screaming at her so much her that my parents dared not leave her alone with him and, although we all wanted Grandma to stay with us permanently, after a few months Mum and Dad felt she had to leave for her own safety. Roy also insisted on eating his meals alone in his bedroom, which upset Mum and Dad greatly because we liked to eat together as a family.

Over time, Roy's behaviour grew even worse and he spent ever longer periods alone in his room. Kerry, who is now an occupational therapist working in Canada, worried that he didn't have any friends and lived in an imaginary world where he often put himself in charge of military battles. Although some days passed calmly, the unpredictability of his moods and his anti-social behaviour kept me on a knife edge of anxiety. I never knew when he was going to start screaming again and hated the stormy and tense atmosphere at home. It was like living with a time bomb. Kerry sometimes locked herself in her bedroom when she heard him shouting and we all felt increasingly scared.

As well as making life difficult for me and Kerry, Roy was also wearing Mum and Dad down. They nevertheless tried to look for positive things about his behaviour and took heart when he visited Uncle Roger, Dad's brother, who lived in a nearby village, because it put him in a better mood. Sadly, once he was back home, he'd usually run up to his bedroom, put a record on and start on his screaming all over again.

He also enjoyed coming on our family weekend camping trips to sites in the North York Moors. We had a large tent with a separate section for each of us. Roy seemed happier in the fresh air, and nothing like as disruptive as he was at home.

Although I was too young to have any real concept of what was going on, I could sense the dark cloud that hung over the family. I was so frightened of Roy's strange behaviour I often shook like a leaf. My parents did their best and took him back to the doctor countless times. They tried a child psychiatrist too, but, as extraordinary as it may seem, his diagnosis remained the same – a bad case of adolescent behaviour – and they were told repeatedly that the best way to deal with their son was to keep reassuring him of their love. Dad even took up kite-flying so that he and Roy could share an activity together, but it failed as Roy would always intentionally get their kites entangled, which was disheartening to Dad, to put it mildly.

One example of his strange behaviour occurred at one of my birthday parties. Dad was in hospital after a fall aboard ship when he'd hit his head on a bulwark, and was expected to stay in for two weeks, but Mum invited twelve little friends round for me and prepared egg, banana and ham sandwiches, jelly and ice cream, and a birthday cake with pink icing. I was very excited but sad too that Dad wasn't with us. It was hard work for Mum to do on her own, but she organized lots of fun games, like Pass the Parcel and Musical Chairs. We were all having a lovely time when, about halfway through the party, Roy came out of his bedroom, walked down the stairs and threw his dinner of meat, potatoes and lots of gravy right across the room. He then started yelling unintelligibly before going back to his room. I was petrified and so upset that my special day was ruined.

Dad's niece Belinda, who had brought her daughter, who was my age, along to join in the fun, was really shocked too. She'd never seen Roy behave like that before and said she'd had no idea that he could be so awful. I could tell Mum was really upset as she cleared up his mess from all over the carpet and armchairs. When everyone had gone home she put me in the bath, read me a story and tried to settle me down for the night. I was still quite disturbed, so it all took a while.

When peace finally reigned, Mum wondered yet again what she and Dad could have done to Roy that he hated them so much, and why such a loving child now seemed like a stranger. She also felt very nervous about what he might do next, but eventually went to bed. She woke up in the small hours with an anxious start, feeling that everything was hopeless. Grandma, whom she loved very much, had died several months previously and she was still in mourning for her. She was also worried about Dad in hospital. It all seemed too much and suddenly she felt she couldn't cope a moment longer. She'd been prescribed Mogadon, a sleeping pill, by the doctor because of the strain she was under and on impulse swallowed all twenty or so tablets left in the container. She left a note on the mantelpiece for Kerry, saying she had gone away, and when we woke up we should all go to our next-door neighbour, whom we knew very well.

She then got into our trusty Morris Traveller and drove off with no idea where she was going. All she knew was that she had to get away. She was not fit to drive and went through several red lights, although luckily there was no one about. Two miles further on the car stalled, which somehow half brought her to her senses. She realized she had to get help, got out of the car and walked unsteadily towards a stationary ambulance parked at the side of the road. The driver got out at the same time and, as fate would have it, it was one of her friends, Billy. When he asked her why she was out in the middle of the night, she told him she had taken an overdose. He immediately drove her to the local hospital in his ambulance, which fortunately was empty.

Mum didn't have to wait long in Casualty. Her stomach was pumped and she was given a bed in one of the wards, but she couldn't sleep and lay shaking and shivering all night. She was in such a state that she didn't think about us poor children left behind, who would wake up with neither parent at home.

Before she was discharged later that morning, she rang a neighbour to ask her to drive her home, and decided not to tell Dad what happened until he came out of hospital. She was in no fit state to go and see him and, so that he didn't worry, left a message with the nurse on his ward that she wasn't very well and couldn't visit him for a couple of days.

When Dad got home he was very shocked and upset to hear what had really happened, but by then Mum was feeling much brighter. Dad had always been an upright, hard-working man who tried to be the husband and father that we could all rely on, but the strain of living with a seriously disturbed teenager was taking its toll on him too. Several days after Mum was discharged, he snapped.

Mum had organized a family Halloween party, hoping Roy would join in the fun. Kerry and I were having a great time, roaring with laughter as we ducked apples and played party games. Roy refused to join in and started annoying us by putting his fingers in his ears and screaming. As we were so used to this by now it wasn't a big deal for us, but it was the last straw for Dad, who broke down in floods of tears. This was so out of character for him that Mum called the doctor, who diagnosed a nervous breakdown caused by stress. He prescribed tranquillizers and Dad took a month off work.

Dad had at that time left the Merchant Navy and had been building up his own electrical business, fixing televisions, radios and the like, and occasionally rewiring houses for friends. It was going very well but Roy's erratic behaviour had become too much for him. He couldn't concentrate on his work and sold the business, which was a pity. Instead he got a job as an electrician at a school in a nearby town, and we bought a four-bedroom semi-detached house close by.

Roy refused to go to school following that incident at my birthday party and, after a nightmare year of having him at home, all our hearts lifted when he suddenly told Mum and Dad that he wanted to follow in Dad's footsteps and join the Merchant Navy. He had been a naval cadet at school and enjoyed it, so we were delighted with his choice. Although we worried a bit about how someone who had such difficulties socially would cope with the other cadets, overall we felt that at long last there was light at the end of the tunnel.

The mood of the house always lifted when Roy wasn't around and this time Mum, who had been so focused on him, started to give us girls, and especially me, more attention. But far from feeling neglected, I enjoyed it when I wasn't the focus of Mum's attention. Instead I had a free, unrestricted childhood, although at times I bubbled over with too much energy and curiosity and was probably a thorn in my elder sister's sides.

Two years after Roy joined the Merchant Navy he was discharged on medical grounds, no doubt because he was acting bizarrely, and our family life once again became a roller-coaster ride. Mum and Dad thought that perhaps he would be happier if we moved to a different house in another part of the Pennines, one that didn't have so many bad memories for him – and for us. So Dad got a job as an electrician at a technical college, and we soon settled into a four-bedroom house in a charming village. Unfortunately the move didn't change Roy's behaviour at all.

I loved being at the new primary school in the village. The teachers were great and made everything fun. I went to Brownies and the Christian Union, enjoyed gymnastics and was quite a tomboy. I had loads of friends, both in the village and at school. I loved climbing trees and fighting with boys but I especially liked going to the local forest to collect the cartridge cases left behind by clay-pigeon shooters. They were all sorts of different colours and I lined them up on the window sill in my bedroom. That summer my friends and I saw a wild horse in a field and the farmer said that whoever could ride it could keep it. We tried all summer but none of us managed to mount the horse, let alone ride it.

Another favourite pastime was our family camping holidays, particularly when our relatives came to join us. Best of all was going fishing with Dad. He was a true family man, a passive and loving father who was very funny and never once smacked me. He had an enduring passion for Austin Minis and, to add to his rather modest income as an electrician, he would often have up to six of them, belonging to various friends, in our garden waiting for him to repair them.

At that time religion wasn't playing a big part in family life. Mum occasionally went to the local Anglican church and even became a Sunday School teacher for a short while, but she found neither peace nor comfort there. Instead both Mum and Dad turned to alcohol as a way of finding relief. They felt better once they were drunk, even though everything became twice as bad the next morning when they were hung-over. On Fridays they drank all night. It was well before the licensing laws changed, so they started at the pub and when it closed they moved on to the nearest hotel with a late-night licence. Dad drank beer and Mum drank white wine. Dad was regularly downing at least eight pints during a session, and by the time he came home he was absolutely reeling and as daft as a brush. He was also chain-smoking and on a Friday would get through about sixty cigarettes during the evening.

Alcohol became Mum's anaesthetic: it helped drown her sorrows and stopped her thinking. I was still young when I became aware that my parents were drinking heavily. Soon after we moved to the Pennine village Mum invited the local vicar to tea. I told him that Mum had been really drunk the previous night. He didn't respond, no doubt because he was trying to be tactful, so

I kept saying it and the more Mum tried to shut me up the more I went on and on. His visit didn't last long.

One of the nicest things about our move was to discover we lived close to a large limestone quarry. As well as being able to play amongst the rocks and pools of the quarry – rather dangerously perhaps, but this was the era before our modern obsession with health and safety – the quarry-workers' families were very friendly and soon began inviting us to various parties. I had countless sleepovers with lots of children in various family bedrooms and it was enormous fun. I was very proud that, although I was one of the youngest there, I was put in charge of making toast for all the children in the morning.

Mum and Dad occasionally went to the local hotel for a posh dinner, and I loved looking at Mum when she was beautifully made up and wearing a smart dress, and thought she was absolutely stunning. When we were at home the family liked to play cards and above all Pit. It's a very old game that simulates the activities on the floor of the stock market, and specifically the commodities market. Everyone would yell out the number of cards they wanted to trade at the same time, and the action was fast and furious. There was so much laughter and shouting going on that I got really cross when my parents sent me to bed, especially as I couldn't sleep for ages because of the noise.

These light-hearted interludes brightened our mood for a short time but didn't provide a permanent solution to the nightmare we had with Roy. He kept thinking people were after him and often woke me at night with his shouting. Although I had my own bedroom I often rushed into my parents' room, where I'd lie on the floor beside their bed, almost too scared to breathe. Sometimes Mum gave me warm milk with a drop of brandy in it to help calm me down. At other times it was really so unpleasant for me to be in our house that Dad called one of our neighbours and asked if I could stay there for the night.

It was around that time that Mum decided once again that life was too much and she couldn't cope with Roy. She'd been secretly going into his room and taking a handful of Valium, which she washed down with sherry, but this time she deliberately took too many and I came home from school to find her flat out on the floor of her bedroom. I was very scared and shook her hard. When she still didn't move, I rang Dad at the college and, after a long wait for him to be found, was eventually put through to him. He rushed home and I stood with my back against the wall in the corner of the bedroom, barely daring to breathe, as I watched him slap her face to try to bring her round. Before long the ambulance arrived and she was taken to hospital. I was completely traumatized by what I had seen and had awful nightmares. Yet I don't think it was a serious suicide attempt. It was more a sign of her desperation and her way of blotting everything out. She was again discharged within a day and not given any medication or a further appointment.

It was the last straw and finally Dad decided, with a heavy heart, that Roy had to move out as he was very worried about the damaging effect his behaviour was having on the rest of us. But it was one thing coming to a decision and quite another finding the courage to tell Roy to his face. He was so volatile it could have easily triggered a serious outburst.

Dad eventually mustered up courage, explained to Roy that he was being rather disruptive and told him gently that he had to go. He added that he was a much-loved son and although we couldn't have him living with us all the time, he wasn't banning him from visiting us. To our surprise Roy wasn't at all bothered and shortly afterwards moved into a squat in a local town that was frequented by homeless people and drug addicts. Life calmed down and one summer's day Roy came round to tell Mum and Dad that he had found what he described as a 'fantastic new church' close to where he was squatting. He asked Mum if she'd like to come with him. She immediately said yes and seemed so happy to find something she could do with Roy that could give them a shared interest and topic of conversation.

Bethesda Charismatic Church was run by Pastor Edmund Collins, a charming, modest young man of 28, who had been building up the congregation from scratch. Mum found her first visit rather strange. She was an Anglican and found the hymns were very different to those to which she was accustomed. The congregation also clapped, which she was not used to. Nor had she ever shouted out 'Halleluiah' before. But the service lifted her spirits and helped her feel peaceful, and she believed that God was there for her to cling on to.

After a few more visits she tried to persuade the rest of the family to join her. Kerry refused, while Dad was so deeply into drink and anti-religion that he said he'd rather spend his time at the pub. But I went along. It was a lovely, lively service, much friendlier than the Anglican church, and I even started going to the Sunday School. Mum became a regular churchgoer and soon wouldn't miss a single Sunday service. She told us that she could sense God's presence within her, felt safe in His hands and suddenly for the first time believed our family would come through our difficult times.

Chapter 3

My Life Is Turned Upside Down

There was an amazing change in Mum once she started going regularly to church. She seemed to cope with life much better and Dad felt he could at last go out with peace of mind, knowing there wouldn't be any more overdoses. Her habits changed too. Mum and Dad regularly went to the pub on a Sunday night, but since Mum found Jesus she usually went to church instead and on the rare occasions she did keep Dad company, she had orangeade rather than white wine.

We all felt better when Mum was calmer and were pleased to see how well she was getting on with Pastor Collins. He told her all about a conference he attended nearby organized by the Divine Congregation, a cooperative fellowship that was spreading the Evangelical message in Britain. He was particularly enthusiastic about Troy Tyson, who he said was a marvellous Canadian missionary who was currently visiting various British churches. He had invited him and another young pastor, Ian Black, whom Tyson had taken under his wing, to speak in the towns and villages of the Pennines. He thought Mum would very much enjoy hearing them preach.

Little did any of us know that this would be an encounter that would change all our lives, and especially mine. Mum went along and was totally absorbed by the service, Black's powerful sermon and the way he singled out individuals, most often women, to pray for their health. She told us she thought he was a wonderful man and very close to Jesus.

Nor was she alone. Rob Jarvis, one of our close friends and usually very down-to-earth, was equally taken with Black, who was, despite the power of his sermons, a short, stocky and sickly looking man. He described Black, who used to work for the Gas Board as a sales manager but who was now an evangelist, albeit with no formal religious qualifications, as someone with a personality that connected with people's search for God and believed that women, in particular, would be captivated by his authority and power and not be bothered that he wasn't particularly good-looking.

Ian Black's first appearance was such a resounding success that he returned each month to preach, staying overnight with various members. Edmund Collins supported him with a good Christian spirit and didn't feel threatened when he heard that Black had created an organization called the Society of Christ's Compassion in the south of England, and was targeting various churches round the country, including his own, to find potential members. And that is why, when Black told him he was organizing a weekend conference down south and had invited several key members of Edmund's church, including my mum, the unwitting pastor encouraged everyone to go along for what he said promised to be a fulfilling Christian experience.

Mum was obviously keen to go to the conference and told us enthusiastically that Pastor Collins believed it would be a place where people could feel the presence of God. She tried to persuade us all to join her, but Dad was indifferent to the offer and turned her down. Kerry said she would travel up from Southampton University, where she was studying occupational therapy, to join Mum. I was happy to be with Mum too. The conference took place in a spacious market hall and there were about 150 of us.

Mum and I loved our time away. We stayed in the home of Celia and Patrick Jones, who were founder members of the Society of Christ's Compassion; they were the parents of a girl, Carol, and the aunt and uncle – and guardians – of Peter, whose parents had been killed in a boating accident some years previously. They made us feel so welcome. Nothing was too much trouble for them and they were really good at putting us at our ease. I immediately hit it off with Peter, who was several years older than me, little thinking that before many years had passed we would become husband and wife.

The highlight of the weekend for me wasn't a religious one, but when Peter, helped by Carol, pushed me in a large old pram at top speed round and round the family's vast garden. Later that day he and I were left alone in the kitchen and ended up having a food fight with some cakes. It all got very silly and Celia was briefly quite angry at the mess we'd made. We quickly apologized.

Mum was really moved by how friendly and loving everyone was. She really took to Celia too, and spent ages pouring her heart out to her about Roy. But most of all she was mesmerized by Black's powerful presence. She found him charismatic and his sermons overwhelmingly authoritative. He told us all that we needed to be where God is and that He had chosen her to be in his church. She believed him and it made her feel special to be there.

I liked the sense of community and the fact that everyone seemed very happy. But I was very scared of Black, particularly when he implied that a local woman, who was an important figure in the Church, had contracted lung cancer because she had criticized Black and that God had given her the illness as a punishment. I was also scared of Black's aloofness and the way he stared at me.

Kerry, who stayed with another couple, was less enthusiastic. She thought Black was distant and cold, and disliked the belittling and intimidating way he talked to her. She also disliked the way the prayer meetings dragged on and on. She wondered whether part of the reason for this was to exhaust the congregation and make them more emotional as a way of putting the fear of God in them and inducing them to become members of the Church. Mum didn't want to hear her criticisms, and came home feeling stronger and more able to cope with her difficult life.

That summer, Roy decided to leave the squat and return to live at home. Initially, we all tried to make him feel welcome and hoped we would be a united and close family again. Tragically his behaviour was even worse than before. He behaved so peculiarly that we were all scared stiff of him. None of us could relax for a second and the tension in the household quickly became unbearable. My parents feared the long-term damage the strange atmosphere would have on us all, and how it would affect our lives as adults. Dad, who had always looked out for us, began to suffer from the same symptoms of stress and panic that had marked the start of his nervous breakdown.

He felt on the verge of collapse and told Mum that if Roy stayed permanently he feared he would become ill again. Mum was beside herself with worry. On impulse she rang one of her friends from Bethesda Charismatic Church, who immediately invited us to come and stay with her family. We accepted her offer and Mum, Dad and I all trooped over and slept in the spare room. It was a crush but at least we felt more sane. After a week Roy was fed up with being on his own and returned to the squat, so we moved back home. The house was in chaos and it took days to get it clean and tidy again.

Unfortunately Roy kept coming back and on one occasion in the middle of the night he went downstairs and turned all of the gas stoves on. Dad, who was an insomniac, smelled the gas and rushed downstairs before anything serious happened. Mum got me out of the house to some other good people from the Church. She and Dad bravely stayed with Roy, and when he calmed down he told them he wanted to move to a larger squat in a bigger town, 'away from small-town life'. In desperation she rang Pastor Collins. Edmund didn't seem to mind how late it was and offered to ask a couple of people from the congregation to drive Roy to wherever he wanted to go. Mum said she would be very grateful, so he rang them immediately. They didn't hesitate to take him on the two-hour car journey. Dad was amazed at their generosity and it ignited something deep inside him.

Roy settled in his new squat and shortly afterwards Dad told Mum he wanted to come to church with her. It was a real turnaround for him, because although he had always considered himself to be a Christian in the way he went about his life, he had been very sceptical about the Church as an institution. He thought it was full of hypocrites who went there when it was good for business. But the way so many of the Bethesda Church members selflessly helped with Roy was a true eye-opener and he was overwhelmed by their kindness. He decided to find out more about this Church, particularly as it was having such a positive effect on Mum.

Dad attended a few services and it wasn't long before he told Mum he could feel that there was someone else in charge and that all situations could be overcome through Him, and that he too wanted to become a Christian. Mum was thrilled and the next time Black came to preach Dad went along to listen. He expected to be very impressed, but was not and instead found him overbearing and insincere. He didn't want to upset Mum as she was going through so much with Roy, so he kept his thoughts to himself.

Mum was meanwhile keeping a much bigger secret from him. At a recent community charity event Black had whispered a few words into Edmund Collins's ear implying that Dad had sexually interfered with me. Pastor Collins quietly passed this information on to Mum, adding that he was sure it wasn't true. Mum knew it was a total lie and although she didn't mention anything to me, she was absolutely right. My wonderful father had never been anything other than appropriately loving towards me.

It was instead an example of Black's trouble-making and his sly way of setting one member of a family against another. Mum kept this dark secret from Dad for twenty years, partly because she knew it was nonsense and partly because she didn't want him to stop being a Christian. Luckily Dad's new-found joy in religion wasn't dimmed by his low opinion of Black, so much so that once he started going to church regularly he found the answers to his prayers. About a year after Roy left to go to his new squat, we were phoned by the police to say he had created such a scene in the street that he had been arrested and sectioned. It had happened before and each time he was taken into hospital he was merely given a dose of some sort of tranquillizer and discharged again.

This time he was again taken to hospital, and Mum and Dad rushed there to see him. When they arrived his first words to them were, 'I am so sorry.' He had never shown any awareness of his effect on the family before and sounded like a totally different Roy. He continued to be so apologetic for all the trouble he had caused that both Mum and Dad burst into tears. Once they calmed down they went to speak to his consultant, who told them that Roy was suffering from bipolar illness. He had been ill for ten years with all the classic symptoms and it was only now that anyone had offered a proper medical diagnosis. They both believed that it was something God had facilitated.

Roy remained in hospital for about a month and was found supported accommodation, where he has lived ever since. He takes mood-stabilizing medication to control his condition and manages his simple life. Support staff help him with daily tasks and activities, and check he is OK. He phones me once a day and my parents about six times, which is sometimes quite stressful for them, but he needs reassurance that we are still there for him.

Once Dad became a committed Christian he stopped both drinking and smoking, and family life dramatically changed as a result of their new religious beliefs. We stopped going to the more riotous parties, gave up playing cards and barely watched TV. Instead my parents' social life revolved around Bible-study groups, going to church and the occasional weekend conference arranged by the Society of Christ's Compassion.

I was still only in my early teens, but the dramatic changes went down like a lead balloon with me. When

Mum went to church before Dad became a Christian she was very discreet about religion and made sure it didn't dominate the house. But suddenly Bibles were everywhere and my parents now played only religious music or recordings of sermons. It was so different from our previous home life and I found it suffocating.

I also felt resentful that they made new rules for me that hadn't applied to my sister Kerry. She had had lots of freedom and fun, but just as I was old enough to join in, everything disappeared. Mum and Dad were trying to get me to go to church all the time, which I certainly didn't want to do. I was so cross that it didn't take long for my rebellious spirit to emerge. In most other households I would have been seen as a fairly typical teenager, but because of what my parents had gone through with Roy, which for years one doctor after another had attributed to youthful rebellion, my general stroppiness seemed far worse than it was.

I had always loved my parents and was basically a decent child, but having endured a pressure-cooker atmosphere at home for so long, I needed to let off steam. Also the change of regime at home, which suddenly switched from being easy-going to strict, occurred at just the wrong time for a lively adolescent girl.

My first teenage rebellion was to become a hippie and I began wearing paisley kaftans, tie-dyed T-shirts and a long Afghan coat that was impregnated with patchouli oil. I also started smoking, like most of my friends. At that time I was a pupil at the local comprehensive school and smoked behind the shed during school hours with a group of friends and, later on, in some derelict woodland once classes were over.

There were some difficult and disruptive children at the school and I knew Mum and Dad were worried about their influence on me. They were right, but the small voice inside me was always aware of what was right and wrong. It was just that at the time it was outweighed by my longing for fun. I started lying to them. I'd say I was staying overnight with a friend and instead went with a gang of about four or five to the woods and stayed up all night drinking and smoking. At about 6 a.m. the next morning we'd all return home bleary-eyed, smelling of fags and cider.

One day as we lay in a clearing in the woods, we made a pact to steal trinkets from the gift shop in the village. It was a ridiculous and horribly dishonest thing to do, not least because the community was very small and everyone knew everyone else. I wanted to back out, but as none of us dared make the first move, I went along too and we all lifted some jewellery. Not surprisingly, a day later a policeman turned up at my home and demanded I hand back what I had taken. I went to my bedroom where I had hidden it all but cheekily decided to give him only half of my haul. Two days later he returned and asked for the rest. This time I handed everything over. My parents were mortified and I was lucky the shop didn't press charges. Instead, Dad took me down to the police station and made me stand in front of the local senior officer, who gave me a severe talking-to. I was very submissive, felt thoroughly ashamed and said I would never do it again.

Even at the time I could tell that my bad behaviour was a reaction to both what had happened at home with Roy and mixing with the wrong crowd. I felt awful about letting Dad down, as he was such a loving father and worked so hard for us. Because of all of this I never shoplifted again. Instead I started playing truant, which I am not proud of either. Mum didn't notice anything when I went out in the morning at the right time in my school uniform but with a pair of jeans or a long skirt stuffed into my satchel. Once I was out of sight I changed direction and met some friends who were also skipping school and we would go off for the day. I even had the cheek to phone the school secretary and, pretending to be my mother, said I had a bad cold and managed to stay away for a week.

Eventually Mum noticed that my school uniform wasn't getting dirty and that I never had any homework. When she challenged me I admitted I had been skipping school. She was so worried about me that she gave up her part-time secretarial job so she could be at home to keep an eye on me. The problem was, I didn't have either the incentive or the discipline to work, as I felt I could never perform as well as my high-achieving sister.

Around this time I started having boyfriends and pretty soon I lost my virginity. I even tried sniffing glue. With a group of friends I went to our woodland haunt where I poured some Tippex correction fluid into a plastic bag and breathed in the fumes. Fortunately, I quickly realized it was a very dangerous thing to do and stopped immediately, although I experienced a brief 'high' followed by a crashing headache. I never tried it again nor touched any other drug, despite my attempt to look and behave like a hippie.

I further disgraced myself when I was invited to a birthday party in a local hall by one of the sixth-form girls at school. I was much younger than nearly everyone else there and when the other guests started dancing I went round sipping their alcoholic drinks. It was a mad thing to do and I ended up being terribly sick in the ladies' loo. My timing was terrible because there was a police raid just as I was throwing up. They were obviously looking for drugs and under-age drinkers, and when they found me in the toilets they rang my father. He came to pick me up but refused to say one word to me during the half-hour drive home. He didn't have to. His look of disapproval was enough. Once we were home he said curtly, 'I will speak to you in the morning, young lady.' I went to bed feeling ill and stupid. Next morning Dad gave me a thorough telling-off. I knew my behaviour had been wrong and I felt ashamed that I had embarrassed my parents.

Mum and Dad remained very worried about me, and although it was obvious that I was not mentally ill, after all they had gone through with Roy they couldn't face another spell of adolescent bad behaviour and the resulting tension at home.

Meanwhile Black's Society of Christ's Compassion was going from strength to strength and had grown to approximately 250 members. He wanted to expand further and so opened a new church building in the south of England, together with a school, in a derelict warehouse on the edge of town. The warehouse was bought with a combination of a large inheritance that Black had recently come into by way of a childless Scottish uncle and donations from nearly all of the church members (Black told his congregation that their gift was a way of thanking God for the blessing of faith). The school was called Tadford School, to tally with the new name that Black had chosen for the church – Tadford Charismatic Church.

That July Mum and Dad decided to go to the church's weekend conference. I didn't want to go as it sounded much too boring but they refused to let me stay at home on my own, or go to a friend. They didn't trust me. I made such a fuss that Mum asked Pastor Collins what she should do. He told her firmly to insist I come too and she told me I didn't have a choice in the matter. I was so furious and upset that I cried throughout the five-hour drive down south to the church. We arrived late on Friday afternoon and pitched our tent in a temporary campsite in an area of wasteland near to the church, which Black used whenever there was a large weekend meeting. It was a grim place and I was still sulky, telling my parents I didn't want to go to any of the Church meetings. Mum said that was OK.

So the next morning I wondered off on my own and had a sneaky cigarette while they were praying. Later that day Mum said Ian Black insisted I come to the evening meeting in the church. I tried arguing but it was hopeless. I trailed along with them to the redeveloped warehouse dressed completely inappropriately. I had put my hippie period behind me and now sported a skimpy black top and very short miniskirt that just about covered my Union Jack knickers, which I had made myself. Inside the warehouse there was a garish floral carpet and row upon row of orange plastic chairs, which were filling up rapidly. There must have been at least three hundred people present. At one end there was a stage and I felt that perhaps we were all going to watch a performance. I was not far wrong.

It was very hot and stuffy in the warehouse-cum-church and I felt very bored. I made the point, as young teenagers do, of making sure my parents knew I didn't want to be there. I refused to stand up when everyone else did to pray loudly or sing. Nor did I join in. Instead I looked around and recognized a few faces from my visit to the Black's previous church with Mum when I was much younger, but I didn't acknowledge anyone. In total contrast to me, my parents were obviously captivated, as were most of the congregation. I must have stuck out like a sore thumb.

We had to go through the same routine on Sunday evening, by which time I was so hot and uncomfortable that I suddenly decided I couldn't take any more. Despite the fact that I was sitting in the middle of a long row and being stared at by Black I got up, squeezed my way through to the end and ran out towards our tent in the temporary campsite. Olivia, who was the wife of the senior pastor, Hugh Porter, ran after me and asked in a doom-laden, intimidating way whether I realized that if I didn't return I would go to Hell. I was so shocked by her words that I started crying and then let her march me straight back into the church again. The entire congregation had seen how I behaved and my parents were obviously very embarrassed.

Black then seized the moment by asking the congregation to pray for me and led the prayers himself. They were all about saving me, not letting me go to Hell and trying to cast out my 'rebellious spirit', which according to 1 Samuel 15:23 is called the sin of witchcraft. I had never been involved in any sort of witchcraft and found the whole thing terrifying. My parents were traumatized too. They knew that to have a daughter labelled as rebellious was a very serious stigma within the Church and kept their heads bowed in shame. I sat quietly next to them, hoping desperately that Black would focus on someone or something else, but when he finished the prayers he said there was someone in the congregation who should go to the new Church school and called out my name.

I couldn't believe what I was hearing and felt a mixture of shock, fury and embarrassment. Black then called me to the front and, with three hundred people's eyes fixed on me, prayed over me yet again. He reeked of Brut aftershave and I really didn't like him. The prayer meeting finished shortly afterwards and I asked my parents what was going on.

Unbeknown to me, my fate had already been sealed the previous day. Mum and Dad had been taken to one side on Saturday morning by Black and the Canadian evangelist Troy Tyson's nephew, Charles, another visiting preacher, and told that they should leave me behind so that I could go to Tadford School. I am convinced the whole thing was premeditated. The school was in its first year and only had fourteen pupils aged between 4 and 18.

My parents were warned by Black and Charles Tyson that my bad behaviour was a certain sign that I was on the road to Hell. They were told that I was in mortal danger unless they moved fast and put me in the care of the Church. It was stressed that there was not a moment to lose and that my situation was so desperate that they shouldn't under any circumstances even take me home with them to collect my things. My only chance of salvation was for me to be left behind immediately.

It was Dad's first visit to Tadford and he decided to talk to Pastor Collins, who was also at the conference, before making such an important and radical decision. Edmund told him it was the best thing that could possibly happen, that it had come from the Lord and was a wonderful opportunity for me. This was a view he later fully acknowledged that he bitterly regretted. Dad's qualms vanished. Not only did he admire Pastor Edmund, but he was also impressed by the Tadford Church members, who he said were the most devoted, loving people he had ever met. He and Mum were shown round the school. It was housed at one end of the warehouse, where swing doors led to the newly built classrooms. Dad was told that Black had started the school in response to the declining Christian, moral and educational standards that were apparent in the state schools.

The Church had a firm Statement of Faith and members were required to believe in a long list of tenets, such as the Virgin Birth, the Second Coming, the depravity of human nature and a number of other things that meant very little to me but which mostly sounded terrifying. Despite my total opposition to the idea, Dad liked the fact that all the teachers were Christians and thought it was a good, clean, godly environment. Although there was something about Black that made Dad feel uneasy and he couldn't warm to him, he decided not to tell Mum and instead tried to put it to one side because he was so impressed by everyone else.

Mum told me that Black suggested I stay at the school for two years and was so persuasive that she and Dad felt that, if they didn't agree, they would be going against what God wanted. I tried to insist I would not change schools, but it soon became obvious that they had made up their minds. I then pleaded with them to take me home so I could collect my things. I had only brought with me what I needed for the weekend, but they refused. I felt frightened, both of being left behind and of all the talk about going to Hell.

My parents stayed on for a couple of days to sort me out for my new life. My miniskirt and tight jeans were completely unsuitable for a Church school and Black told Mum to take me shopping in town for some new clothes. I ended up with a small selection of ghastly, demure three-quarter-length skirts and dresses, long-sleeved blouses with high necks and thick stockings, all of which were designed to make me look respectable and modest. I was not allowed to have jeans or trousers because Black apparently believed they were not lady-like. I hated everything, and felt I was losing my indi viduality. Instead of being a distinctive teenager I looked like Mary Poppins.

But I didn't make a terrible scene. It was all much too serious and I was in shock. Instead, I did what I was told and behaved like a robot. After our shopping trip Mum and I came back to the church to buy the school uniform. This consisted of a grey pleated skirt with a white blouse, a maroon blazer with grey trim to match the skirt, a grey coat and a maroon hat, also with a grey trim. It was all hideous. I felt terribly upset that I was not allowed to go home to say goodbye to my friends or boyfriend, who I was particularly keen on, or collect my books, diary and special things.

My parents left on Wednesday morning and I was in floods of tears as they hugged me and said goodbye. I have since learnt that lots of questionable organizations, selling anything from double glazing and commemorative china to religion, often target people and pressurize them into making quick commitments. They persuade them that, unless they make a fast decision, they will lose the chance to take advantage of whatever is on offer.

But, at Tadford on that bleak Sunday in July when my fate and future were about to be sealed, neither of my parents felt under duress, nor were they the slightest bit suspicious of any ulterior motive on the part of Black. Mum had looked round the school, seen well-mannered children and thought that it would be the ideal thing for me. She had always wanted me to have the best opportunities in life and thought that here was my chance.

For my parents it was a hard decision and a sacrifice to leave me behind, both emotionally and financially. Mum even went back to work full-time to pay for my schooling. She also told Black that she wanted me to come home during half-term and the school holidays, and at most stay for a year, but I didn't know that. Nor did she realize I would be one of only two boarders.

In the cold light of the long car journey home, neither of them felt quite so confident about what they had done. Mum felt guilty and inadequate at not being able to manage me, and about passing me on to somebody else what she felt was really her problem. Dad just felt terrible. They talked about what had happened all the way back. Neither of them slept that night, while several hundred miles away I cried myself to sleep.

Chapter 4

Handed Over to Tadford

I felt totally felt bereft as I watched my parents drive off. My bolshie, know-it-all attitude disappeared and I yearned for Mummy and Daddy to stay with me. I didn't feel nearly ready to stand on my own two feet and worried that the strange, restricted new world I suddenly found myself in would prove a very lonely place. It didn't help that after my parents left I discovered that I was one of only two boarders. My heart sank. I couldn't believe it. I thought that at least there might be the possibility of some late-night fun with other girls in a dormitory. Instead I was told I was going to live in Ian Black's house with his family.

Ian Callum Fitzroy Black was born in 1939, the son of a prosperous Scottish banker. His father died in the North African campaign fighting for Monty and the Eighth Army when he was 3 and, after being looked after by his mother until he was 8, he was sent off to a private school in the Scottish Highlands, where his father had been a pupil. After leaving school he worked on a large Highland estate as a trainee forester, but, finding that he was less than keen on such a solitary life in the wet wilderness of the Scottish mountains, he soon moved to England in search of work.

For a while he found employment selling agricultural machinery to farmers in Lincolnshire, but, again dissatisfied with his lot, he eventually ended up as a Gas Board employee, becoming a regional sales manager within a couple of years. A dramatic change occurred in his life at his mother's funeral. Black, who previously had not given much thought to religion or to God, was devastated by his mother's death and at her funeral, wracked with grief, suddenly understood the meaning behind the arcane symbols and rituals of the Church.

Shortly after this epiphany, Black met Heather, a librarian from Stamford, at a party thrown by one of his colleagues. Initially, the two were friends, but their relationship soon developed and they were married in Lincoln a year after they first met. They moved to a small town nearby, where Black became involved with the local church, taking on the role of lay preacher. Several years later they moved south, where he was able to take up another position with the Gas Board, and bought a rambling six-bedroom house with a large garden.

During this period he started prayer meetings with Heather and another couple, David and Charlotte Snelling, whom they met at church. Others gradually joined them and when there were about seventy regulars they decided to formalize the group. They called themselves the Church of Christ's Compassion. Shortly afterwards, Black met the Canadian evangelist preacher Troy Tyson, who took him under his wing.

Black and his wife had five children – Ione, Callum, Lucy, Helen and James – and one boarder, a girl some years younger than me called Angie, who was also a pupil at Tadford. I was told that I had to share a room with her. She was sweet and bubbly and had a good sense of humour, but although the difference in our ages was not that big, the difference in our likes and dislikes was enormous. Angie's bedroom was decorated in pink and very girly, but from the start I could tell she didn't want to share it with me and I didn't blame her. Who would want a stranger suddenly turning up without warning who took up space in a room you'd previously had to yourself? But that's what happened. Black and his wife, together with Angie, had driven to Greece 'on business' the day before my parents left, and Alex and Siobhan Scott, a newly married couple who were also founder members of the Church, moved in to look after us. Siobhan taught in the Church school, while Alex was a manager at the local printer's.

I felt terribly homesick and totally traumatized by what had happened. From being the baby of the family and secure in my parents' unconditional love, I had been dramatically uprooted and deposited in what felt like an alien land. And I'd had no time to prepare myself either psychologically or physically. I hadn't said goodbye to any of my many friends. I felt like an amputee who had not only lost all her limbs but had had her heart torn out as well. I had no coping mechanism. I was no longer a child and not yet a woman. Not surprisingly, at first I cried a huge amount. I also wrote to some of my friends telling them I was trapped and asking if they could smuggle me some cigarettes. I didn't really want the cigarettes: it was just my way of connecting with my friends without losing face. They posted several packets to me but I didn't smoke them. You weren't allowed to and I was frightened of getting caught and what the punishment might be.

When Black returned from his trip, Angie insisted she wanted her room back. Black told me he would get the builders in to alter his house to accommodate me in another room and that in the meantime I would be living with Alex and Siobhan in their home. It seemed rather odd to alter his house for one pupil but he seemed determined to have me live there. I had no idea why. Alex and Siobhan lived in a ground-floor flat in the town where the Church had originally started, several miles from Tadford and Black's house. It was another upheaval for me, especially as there was no one to help smooth my way. I felt totally lost and abandoned.

Siobhan was strict, which was fair enough. She probably found it just as difficult living with a young teenager as I did living with a new family. She often became quiet and distant, and it was difficult to know where I stood with her. Alex, on the other hand, was funny and cracked jokes to ease any tension in the home. He also cooked fantastic pizzas and regularly bought us samples of the comics that his company printed. Between them, it seemed to me, they controlled everything in my life and never allowed me to be on my own. I felt as if I were in a prison and was so unhappy that I refused to unpack for a long time after I moved in.

Inevitably the atmosphere in the flat was tense as every day I'd tell Alex and Siobhan that I wanted to go home. I'd tell my parents the same thing every time they rang me. I was allowed to call them every other day but I noticed that either Alex or Siobhan would hover in the background while I was on the phone, perhaps to hear what I was saying. My phone calls were always the same. I'd plead with them to come and get me, and tell them how much I hated Tadford. Mum and Dad would then both say they wouldn't come, that I was there for my own good and that everything would be fine because there were so many people at the Church who loved me.

Then I'd cry, '*Please, please,* let me come home,' and even though I could tell Mum was upset hearing me cry, she kept saying, 'No, you can't.' The phrase 'hitting your head against a brick wall' kept coming to mind. The more I tried to convince my parents I was in a place that was nothing like the caring community they imagined, the less they seemed to listen. I felt instinctively that it all had dark undertones but I somehow couldn't put it into words. I certainly didn't tell them that during Church assemblies we were encouraged to forget our past and think of the Church as our family, even though to my young ears it sounded totally disloyal.

Mum would say things like boarding school is always very difficult for a child during the first few weeks and homesickness is very common. She told me she thought I'd soon get used to it once I made friends. Her responses sounded rather prepared and it crossed my mind whether this was what she had been told to tell me. But I knew it wouldn't be fine and my fear was confirmed when I went to school for the first time a week after I arrived. It had been hard enough for me to conform to the comparatively free-and-easy school routine at my local comprehensive, but the narrow, restricted and unimaginative curriculum at Tadford School was mind-blowingly boring.

The school day started with religious assembly at 8.15 a.m., followed by lessons. I had been used to a large, open classroom full of children of my own age, all chatting and working together. Now, because there were so few of us, most of the time we were lumped together in one classroom. The younger children sat down one side of the room and older ones like me down the other, and woe betide any child who even tried to look at another. We were so repressed we weren't allowed to speak during lessons, during meal breaks, or even when we were changing for games.

Despite being deeply shocked, I tried to analyse my situation. On the one hand, I felt it was far too cruel a punishment for someone whose only wrongdoing was to be a rather boisterous teenager. On the other hand, I never doubted that my parents loved me and wanted the best for me. It was all too confusing and I didn't know where to turn.

Initially the school followed a Christian method of home teaching that basically meant self-learning. This was totally new for me and I missed the stimulation of having other children around me with whom I could share thoughts and ideas. Instead, each of us had our own individual work to do. I was given a work book which set questions, exercises and essays, and when I had finished one set I had to go to a table in the middle of the room, find the book of answers and mark my own work. I then went back and did the next exercise. If any of us needed help from the teacher we had to hold our hand up, and when, eventually, the teacher saw it she would come to help us.

It was all so excruciatingly dull that I used to keep falling asleep. The only thing that slightly cheered me up – proof that I desperately needed even the smallest crumb of comfort that could link me with my family – was the small Tony the Tiger I put on my desk, which I'd bought with my mother just before she left.

One of my worst tasks was to learn 'memory verses'. This required pupils to learn a different set of twelve verses from the Bible every week. I'd never done anything like it before and was so hopeless at it that sometimes Black rebuked me in front of the whole school, telling everyone that I hadn't made an effort and I should try harder. He turned up at school assembly about once a month and usually called someone up on to the stage for an alleged misdemeanour. Sometimes it would be a pupil who had showed what he called 'an improper attitude'. At other times it was someone like me who didn't do well with the memory verses. Although many of us cried, I didn't dare discuss his behaviour with anyone else, and if it was an attempt to humiliate me, it worked every time. I felt useless and stupid, and this only served to highlight my chronic loneliness.

At lunchtime the older ones like me had to turn into dinner ladies and help dish up the meal to the other pupils, then wash up all the plates and cutlery by hand afterwards. Although there was a dishwasher in the kitchen, it was never used. I'd had to help out at home, but it had been a family thing, and we'd chat and laugh as we did the washing up or laid the table. Now I resented it, especially as everything had to be cleared up before I could go out to play. At my previous school I always had loads of girls to play with, but at Tadford there were only two other girls of my own age. Luckily I did enjoy the interaction between children of different ages and often played skipping games with the little ones.

There was always plenty of food to eat, but there was no choice and this led to my first confrontation with Black, shortly after he returned from Greece. The meal was Lancashire hotpot and the last time I'd had it – well before I was at Tadford – I was violently sick. There had obviously been something wrong with the meat but I'd decided I didn't want to eat Lancashire hotpot ever again. Unluckily it was on the school menu on a day he came round to check that we were all eating – in fact he always seemed to be everywhere I went – and he asked me why I was leaving it. I explained what had happened and he replied that it was compulsory at Tadford to eat every-thing that was put in front of me. I refused and he told me I couldn't leave the dining room until I had. I showed my fighting spirit by arguing with him for two solid hours until he instructed me to leave the meal on the table and come to his house. We went to the lounge, where Black, plus the head of the school, his secretary Charlotte Snelling, his spokesperson Siobhan Scott and his wife Heather, all key members of the Church, had already gathered. I don't know if he had summoned them, but the argument was quickly established as five of them against one of me. I kept saying, 'I am not eating it.' They kept telling me, 'Yes you are.' It continued for another hour until finally I suddenly felt so worn down I burst into tears and agreed to go back and eat the hotpot. It was stone-cold and, in its puddle of congealed grease, tasted disgusting. I wasn't physically sick but the damage that being forced to eat it did to my spirit was substantial.

Black and the others had won the battle and perhaps felt triumphant that my will had been broken. It was clearly something they considered much more important than my missing an afternoon of school. I, on the other hand, was left feeling emotionally battered, alone and trapped in a place where I didn't want to be. I did, though, win another confrontation. When the builders finished partitioning Angie's room at Black's house and he told me that the new room was now going to be mine, I dug my heels in and absolutely refused to move in. Nothing would budge me and in the end I was allowed to remain with Siobhan and Alex. It was a massive relief, because he still terrified me.

On Wednesdays I had only morning school because I had to help cook, serve and wash up for the weekly group lunch of teachers and other Church staff. One adult and I were involved in catering for about ten of them, including Black, and I absolutely hated doing it. All the other children went home and after the elected adult had cooked everything, she went home too, leaving me on my own to serve, clear up, and wash and dry everything. Perhaps I was chosen because, apart from Angie – who was considered too young – I was the only boarder and didn't have a real home to go to, which in itself made me feel very bad. I used to find it exhausting and didn't finish until about 4 p.m. I had school on Saturdays, too. Mornings consisted of classes in dressmaking, which I was useless at, typing and cooking. Black had the idealistic, old-fashioned attitude that women were at their best in the home catering for a man's every need and believed they should be taught the necessary skills from a young age. In the afternoon I had to play table football. I also learnt badminton and netball.

Normally school finished at 3.45 p.m. and I didn't do much afterwards, apart from going food shopping with Siobhan and doing my homework. I thought longingly of my gang of friends and how we used to run off laughing together into the woods, or just chill out somewhere and chat non-stop. Now I had nothing to do, no one to do it with and no one to talk to. I felt bereft. I used to talk about anything and everything to my friends, but now my life both in and out of school was largely lived in silence. Although my parents paid full fees for my education, I had to do all the chores for nothing. As well as the Wednesday lunch, after table football on Saturday afternoon I had to help clean the entire school and before Church services I had to clean the toilets, vacuum the enormous church hall and set up the chairs. I thought of it all as slave labour.

Soon after I started at the school, Black instigated a 7 a.m. prayer meeting. It was way too early. I didn't want to go but I had to, so I dozed throughout. Luckily these sessions were stopped after a few months, I imagine partly because of the ridiculous hour and partly because Black didn't like small or private gatherings as he wasn't in control of them.

Right from the start the thing I dreaded most about Tadford was being summoned into Black's private office. It was called 'the private haven' and I feared it because he repeatedly made me feel useless, unworthy and full of despair. My first visit came shortly after the Lancashire hotpot episode. His manner was almost immediately intrusive and within minutes he asked me if I had had sex and if I was pregnant. I was shocked by such crude and personal questions and didn't want to answer him, but he kept asking me, and in the end I didn't have the maturity or confidence to tell him it was a private matter and found myself confessing instead. I told him that I had had sex, but that I always used protection and wasn't pregnant. He then asked me lots of questions about my social life, about what I did and where I went. By the end of it all I felt thoroughly dirty, exposed and humiliated, that what I had done was terribly wrong and that there was no hope for me at all. This one dressing-down also had a long-term effect. It made me feel sex was wrong even if it had been sanctioned by a wedding and I don't think Peter and I ever experienced true physical intimacy. Despite my huge embarrassment, somewhere at the back of my brain I noted that Black seemed to almost relish the process of breaking me down and extracting my confession.

He then insisted I write to my parents telling them when I had lost my virginity and that I had lied to them about going to a party. I did what I was told without thinking too much about how my unnecessary letter would upset them. That hit me when my father replied. He wrote:

> *I feel very hurt that you should find it necessary to lie and deceive me ... You should know by now that you only get away with a lie for so long then it catches up on you. As I said I feel terribly hurt. I don't know*

what else will be revealed, however because we love you so much we forgive you for everything that has happened in the past.

There is one thing for certain you could not come back and carry on as you were, it is with this in mind that I must insist that you stay at Tadford as far as we are concerned from now on the past should be forgotten. If you feel you would like to make amends for what has happened the best way you can do it is by really working hard and build a good future for yourself so that in the future you too will have the choice of going to university the same as Kerry if you want to …

The letter was a crushing blow. Dad was such a gentle man and the harsh, unbending tone was so unlike him that I immediately wrote him another letter of apology. At the end of October I received his reply:

Your first letter took a lot of courage to write and tells me that I now have a daughter who has matured and is now going the right way in life, with regards to its contents of course we forgive you because we love you so much.

Our love is even stronger now because you have been so honest with us. As regards to anything else we may find out, these too will be forgiven.

If you remember some time back I had a talk with you and I said there was a battle going on inside you with two people, one was the Devil himself and the other was that loving person with that lovely personality.

The battle is now over and I thank God for my lovely loving daughter has won. You can now look forward to a future full of happiness and love, as for ourselves our prayers have been answered in full. I agree with you that it is a lousy world for teenagers to grow up in.

God bless you my darling and here are lots of sloppy kisses.

Mum and Dad xxxxxxxxxxx

I felt very mixed emotions when I received this letter. I was pleased Dad seemed to have forgiven me, but it made me realize that my life at Tadford was a done deal and that there would be no reprieve. It was a long time before it dawned on me that my parents had absolutely no need to hear explicit details about my sex life. Children don't tell their parents what they get up to. It is totally inappropriate and unnecessary, and the pressure on me to confess all was, I came to believe, more about driving a wedge between us than setting any sort of record straight.

Shortly after my problems with the hotpot I had another run-in with the teachers. I was supposed to go swimming in the town swimming baths, but my period, which had previously stopped for about a year – I'm not sure why – started again. I was in a lot of pain and absolutely didn't want to swim. I felt too embarrassed to explain the real reason and instead just kept refusing to go. Siobhan Scott, who was with me in the corridor of the new school building, got very cross and eventually Heather Black was asked to come over. Even though she was quite a tall woman of substantial build, it seemed to me she did everything her much smaller husband told her to do.

She was furious at my refusal and started to try to drag me to Black's office, but I broke away and ran out of the school, my only thought being that I had to get away. It was totally impulsive. I had no specific place to go to or any sort of plan. Tears streamed down my face and even though I didn't have any money on me, I stopped at the nearest bus stop hoping a bus might come that I could jump on to and escape. A woman was waiting for the bus and must have wondered what on earth was going on. Heather caught me before a bus arrived and marched me straight to the house where she and her husband lived. We went into Black's study, where a number of important Church members, including Charlotte Snelling and Olivia Porter, were waiting.

The room was dark and had a distinct smell of leather. There were two red leather sofas, a big brown leather chair and lots of books lining the walls. I was told to sit on one of the sofas and Siobhan sat next to me. I was then bombarded with accusations of how rebellious and terrible I was, and each person told me in turn that I had to do what I was told. The telling-off lasted about two hours, most of which I spent in tears. I finally confessed that I had my period and that was why I couldn't swim. They all looked at me incredulously and started laughing. Black asked if that was all and hadn't I ever heard of a Tampax? I thought it was an awful thing to say to a young teenage girl who had just arrived in a completely new place. I didn't know how to reply or why a group of adults would want to gang up on a young person. So I just sat speechless, feeling a mind-numbing embarrassment that stayed with me for weeks. As did my hatred of Black and how wretched he made me feel.

When they finally let me go, I went straight to Siobhan's house, phoned my parents and pleaded with them once again to take me away. I was too inhibited to tell them about the Tampax incident and only spoke in general terms, saying yet again how much I hated the place. Not surprisingly they said I should stay and they would see me soon. I felt crushed and hurt. I had to do everything in my power to escape its grip. Quickly, before it was too late. I had never felt so alone, so unloved and so full of emotional pain. But no matter how loudly I shouted for help, no one, not even my parents, listened. Mum and Dad seemed united in taking the same hard line. There was no give and take. I couldn't negotiate with them an inch. The bald reality was that I was imprisoned in a place I loathed. Was this what I deserved? Was I so awful? Yet even in the depths of my pain I managed to separate the knowledge that my parents wanted me from the fact that they couldn't cope with a feisty teenager.

When I put the phone down I thought, 'I just can't feel any worse', and as the days went by I simply couldn't settle. I felt desperate and scared. I had to escape, so a few days later I tried to run away again. I had no particular plan. All I could focus on was escaping. My parents had regularly sent me pocket money for toiletries and snacks, none of which I had been allowed to spend. When I counted it all up I realized I had £16. It was enough, I decided, to catch the bus at the end of the street and get away. I packed a small bag, slipped out of the house in the early afternoon and started walking down the street. A little old lady, a member of the Church, stopped me and started talking. It seemed rude not to listen and she chatted for so long that by the time we went our separate ways, I chickened out and went back.

Later that same week I made another half-hearted attempt to escape. This time I waited until 1 a.m. to make sure Alex and Siobhan were asleep. I put on a pair of drainpipe jeans I had brought with me when I originally came for the conference and which I had managed to keep hidden when all my unsuitable clothes were taken away. My plan was to climb out of the ground-floor window rather than risk using the front door. I lowered my bag down with a hockey stick that was being stored in my room, but when I tried to get out of the window I got caught on the latch, half in and half out. At that moment a police car drove very slowly down our road.

Alex and Siobhan lived in a small street off the main road and I thought the police must have spotted me from the top of the road and come to investigate. I panicked, somehow managed to wrench myself back into the room, and waited very quietly with my heart pounding until they drove away. I was frightened of what would happen to me if they caught me. Suddenly I also became aware that I could be struck down by God if I escaped. So I fished up my bag, got undressed and went back to bed. These experiences showed me the difference between the theory of wanting to get away and the practice of doing so.

The Church's seemingly deliberate process of demoralizing me and breaking my spirit continued relentlessly.

I had to go to services about four nights a week and on Wednesday nights Black often homed in on individuals and called them to the front of the stage. He called me far too often and prayed loudly over me, saying things like, 'In the name of Jesus I cast out this rebellious spirit.' The sign of a rebellious spirit, as far as Black was concerned, could be as minor as my questioning something he said. I realized it was one of the ways he could give me a dressing-down in public, and it always worked. I never failed to feel humiliated and embarrassed. Others were called up for any of a whole range of reasons, including some that were unbelievably trivial

As well as undermining my character, Black also criticized my family. He would say my parents were a bad influence on me and that they were the reason for all my problems, that my sister and brother were going to Hell, that I was the only member of my family that God had chosen for salvation, that I now had a new family, God's family, and that I should forget my old family.

He didn't put me off Mum and Dad. If anything he made me more desperate to get home to them. But I couldn't even mention going home without someone in authority telling me that if I did go I would receive seven evil spirits, that I would go to Hell, that God would strike me down and I would become a drug addict, all of which stems from Matthew 12:43–5. I felt everything I did was wrong and awful. I lost my self-esteem, felt dirty and full of sin, and yearned to be hugged and loved. I kept thinking about my Dad and what a loving man he was, and how I used to sit on his knee and cuddle up to him when we watched the news on television together.

Despite what we had gone through with Roy, we were a close family and I missed the intimate contact with my parents, sister and my friends, most of whom must have thought I had disappeared into thin air. I took some consolation from knowing that at least my parents loved me regardless of what I did, whereas at Tadford any love was dependent on my conforming and doing exactly what I was told. I also knew that my parents' priority was for me to get a good education. Unfortunately, they were taken in by the Blacks and the respectable, well-mannered children. I think they were rather naive in not feeling suspicious about how heavily they were pushed to make a quick decision about me. It didn't help that Pastor Edmund, whom they admired and trusted, encouraged them. Perhaps he did so on the basis of Black's unfounded insinuation that there was something not quite right about my relationship with my father. I was pleased when he later apologized for having been taken in by Ian Black.

* * *

As the autumn nights shortened and the days drew in I comforted myself with the thought that Christmas would soon arrive and, although I was not allowed to go home for the holiday, my parents would be coming to see me. I remained hopeful that I would be able to persuade them to take me home.

I had no idea that my parents had expected me to come home during my first half-term break and that they were very disappointed not to see me. They thought it best not to tell me that one of the Church elders had informed them that I couldn't come back because new boarders needed to stay for a certain period to acclimatize, and that any such visit would be too disturbing and make it difficult for me to settle back in again. At last my parents arrived, just before Christmas, laden with presents, and were really pleased to be with me again. They were also keen to see for themselves how I was settling down and whether the wholesome atmosphere was doing me good. I had no patience with that and straight away asked them to take me home permanently. They tried to calm me without promising anything. The following day they went to a pre-Christmas meeting in the church. At the end of the meeting Black went up to them and told them bluntly that Kerry had an evil spirit, the same evil spirit as Roy, and would go to Hell. Mum was horrified, not least because he hadn't even met Kerry, but she didn't say a word to me. Dad immediately told Black that she most certainly did not have an evil spirit, but his comments totally ruined their Christmas.

The routine at Tadford Charismatic Church was that all members and guests would eat a Christmas lunch together several days before Christmas as one great family, and that year over two hundred people sat down to a traditional meal of turkey and all the trimmings at a local hotel. It was the job of Church members who were single and between the ages of 14 and 40 to prepare, cook, lay the tables, serve the meal and wash up afterwards, and on this occasion there were about thirty of us. Unfortunately, I woke up on the day of the lunch feeling really unwell and felt increasingly poorly as the day went on, until, as the meal was being served, I went to another hotel where my parents had been staying to lie down. Shortly afterwards Mum and Dad came to see me. They had lost their appetites after Black's comment about Kerry and couldn't wait to leave the table. I told Mum, in a rather dramatic fashion, that I thought I was dying and asked her to call the doctor. She asked Siobhan, who had come round to the hotel to see what the problem was, what she thought and said to her in front of me that she believed I was putting it on. She then told me to stop being manipulative and behave myself. I had a restless night, with a hacking cough and a raging temperature, and felt so ill that even wearing clothes hurt my skin. Siobhan then rang the GP, who came round to see me. He asked if I had a rash and I told him I had blotches all over my skin. He examined me and diagnosed measles.

Mum and Dad were in Black's office when the doctor came. They had been summoned there, and assumed he was going to give them a progress report on my school work. To their absolute astonishment, instead he told them what he had previously told me: that they were the cause of my problems and they should go away and forget they had ever had me. He added he didn't want any more communication between my parents and me. He failed to mention at all how I was doing at school, and Dad was so furious he came back to Siobhan's house and told me that he and Mum were so appalled by what he had said that they had decided I could come home for good after all. I couldn't believe it and made him repeat the news twice. Despite feeling really unwell, I was elated. Sadly, before they did so they felt it would be wise to speak to the doctor to check if I was all right to travel.

My original GP wasn't called, and instead a doctor who was a member of the Church came to see me and said I was far too sick to be moved. I knew I was ill but I felt I could be given some paracetamol and sleep in the back of the car wrapped up in a duvet. Even in my ill state I suspected that the doctor had been told what to say by Black. Unfortunately my parents didn't want to risk my health and said they would have to leave me behind. They felt they were caught between a rock and a hard place, and didn't know what to do for the best. So, once again, before they made a final decision they took their dilemma to Pastor Collins. Apparently he told them that I would have a good education at Tadford and be in good company, and that we should all ignore Black's less attractive comments. I know, too, that they were concerned that if I did come home I might go back to partying all the time and perhaps even take drugs. So on balance they decided to leave me where I was.

I wondered whether my parents, along with other members of the Church, also assumed I had developed measles as God's way of keeping me there. I was broken-hearted that my parents left without me and I stayed in bed for about a week. Just as I was beginning to feel better, Black told me that from September, when I started my O Level course, I was not going to be allowed to phone my parents except on Christmas Day and birthdays. Apparently my parents were given the same instruction, with the explanation that lack of contact would enable me to concentrate fully on my school work. Luckily we could write to each other.

I don't know the exact moment when I stopped listening to my inner voice and began to conform, but round about then my actions and behaviour became increasingly governed by fear. When Black preached he implied time and time again that if I walked away from Tadford something terrible would happen to me. I began to believe him and felt sure that if I left I would indeed go to Hell. He kept repeating that Roy was possessed, which is why he had bipolar disorder, and that Kerry was heading the same way. He insisted that the members of Tadford were my family now, my only hope and where the light was, and that I must follow this light just as the children of Israel followed the pillar of fire in the desert.

He was careful not to say directly that if any of us left we would die. Instead he referred to ex-members' deaths as being a result of their no longer being of the Church or giving their life to God. We all knew what he meant. I believed him because I was young and scared.

Chapter 5

All Work and No Play

After my parents left I accepted my fate and resigned myself to being at Tadford. I wrote to them each week and they in turn tried to keep me up to date with the nitty-gritty of family life. I read each of their letters several times and kept them all. Some of them sounded quite sad and I could tell they missed me.

Life with Alex and Siobhan became relatively peaceful but it was extremely dull. My days were taken up with school, homework and church. If I wasn't praying I was cleaning something or washing up. I had no social life at all and there was no chance for me to make any friends outside of school. I wasn't allowed to go to the cinema or cafés, like any normal teenager, and certainly not to a disco. I had never known such endless boredom, nor such a feeling of isolation. The contrast with the life I had once enjoyed couldn't have been more different.

How ironic, I thought, that like many normal teenage girls I had complained to my parents about my lack of freedom and pushed against the boundaries, but now it had been taken away I appreciated how much freedom I'd really had. At home I could come and go with my friends whenever I wanted. I always had someone to talk to and lots to do, and was never short of a friend to go to the cinema with. Now everything in my life took place within the strict control and orbit of the Church. I wasn't even allowed to go home during the school holidays. Instead, I was given piles of holiday homework, plus menial jobs to do for the Church to keep me busy. I had always been a gregarious child, but with no outlet for my personality I felt I was shrivelling up inside.

Six months after my parents left me I had an unexpected visit from Kerry. I was really pleased to see her, but we were not allowed to be alone and couldn't talk properly. Siobhan or another Church member stayed close to me to make sure I behaved and didn't say anything I shouldn't. Part of me was pleased to see Kerry as a link to the family, but on the down side her presence highlighted my plight and how much I missed home. Nobody loves or hugs you like your parents and siblings. It also frustrated me that I couldn't talk naturally, let alone confide in her, because I was so closely chaperoned. As a result I just didn't know what to say to her.

Kerry stayed only a few hours and I think she found me very subdued and not at all like the lively young sister she once knew. She told me many years later that she had been hoping to help me get away but found it impossible to even broach the subject. After she left I came to the conclusion that communicating with my family broke my heart and caused me so much agony that the best thing I could do was get my head down and work. And apart from the odd rebellious moment, that is what I did. It helped that Black was travelling around the world a lot of the time, to bring Jesus to the masses, and not hovering over me. When he wasn't around sermons were usually given by his deputy, Hugh Porter.

About twice a year all of us who were over 14 had to fast for a whole weekend and could drink only water. It was seen as a way of clearing the system and concentrating on godly things. Instead of eating, we spent whole days in the church. Each day seemed like a year as I sat through endless prayers, sermons and more prayers, with only short breaks in between. I managed to sneak in some peppermints to suck but they didn't help much with my hunger pains. The Easter weekend was the worst. The plan was to spend three solid days in church fasting and praying. The fast was over after the Sunday morning service and I was so hungry that when I got home I demolished in one go all the Easter eggs I had been given. I felt terribly sick afterwards.

At the start of each summer holiday all the school pupils from the age of 4 upwards went on a summer camp. That year we went to a campsite close to Lyme Regis in Dorset. We pitched our tents and I was in one with a fellow pupil about my age and three little ones. The holiday wasn't much fun, especially when Black was there. Every morning and evening we had to attend religious meetings where we were supposed to feel what he described as God's Holy Spirit, and he prayed that we would be saved and brought to Christ. We were encouraged to shout and scream that we believed in Christ, and at times the noise and emotion were so overwhelming that most of us, but not me, cried.

On the second day Black told us that everyone over the age of 10 had to go on a twelve-mile walk. There was no choice of activity: that was what we had to do whether we liked it or not. I didn't like the idea and told him so. He wasn't pleased. None of us was allowed to question him and he accused me of having 'a bad attitude'. Nobody confided that they agreed with me. We were always guarded with each other and it was frowned upon to stand out from the crowd.

In the evenings we didn't sing jolly songs round a campfire or have time to muck about like kids usually do. Instead we had the prayer meeting, then a cup of Ovaltine, and were told to go to sleep at about 10 p.m. I hated having a fixed bedtime. It made me feel like a child rather than a young woman.

At school I followed the Church education scheme for nine months, then, when most pupils in the country were taking their O Levels, I was allowed to switch syllabuses and start work on mine. I had no choice in the matter and was told I would take eight subjects. I had by now spent a quietish year at school, and although I wasn't allowed to go home, I had made friends with other girls of various ages and felt slightly more comfortable.

After my O Levels I officially left school and thought carefully about what I should do with my life and what career path to follow. I was by now thoroughly institutionalized and had grown into a narrow-minded, docile and prissy young woman. Black was keen for Church members to work and earn well so that they would be in a position to give funds to the Church. After careful consideration I decided I would like to become a social worker. Normally young teenagers would discuss their idea with their parents. But this wasn't encouraged at Tadford. We were supposed to see the Church leaders as our family and talk to them instead. So before I could do anything constructive with my choice I had to make an appointment to see Black and ask his permission.

I always felt sick and anxious when I went into his office, in case I got another telling-off, but I had no choice. He greeted me in his familiar, rather overbearing and patronizing way, and looked aghast when I told him I wanted to do my A Levels and then take a degree in social work. At the time the school didn't offer a range of A Level subjects, because there weren't many sixth-form pupils, but I hoped I might be given permission to go to a local sixth-form college. When I finished speaking he stared at me in silence for what seemed like hours but was probably only a couple of minutes. My heart was pounding as I waited for his answer. He kept his gaze fixed on me, then said in his firm, loud voice that I must forget my plan as I wasn't intelligent enough to be a social worker or study for a degree. I had never thought of myself as being very intelligent, particularly when I compared myself with Kerry, who by that time had just embarked on a doctorate in occupational therapy.

In theory I could have walked out of Tadford and made a new life for myself. But the thought didn't enter my mind. If it had, I wouldn't have dared to pay attention to it. It would have made Black furious, and therefore God as well, and the consequences would have been too awful to contemplate. My self-esteem, along with my extrovert nature, had long gone, so I assumed his judgement about me was right and he was merely confirming everything he had always said about me being hopeless. He told me he felt I should find a job in

London instead. I was then dismissed. It was the sum total of my career advice. He didn't tell me what sort of job I should try for or give me even the basic practical details of how you go about finding a job. It was strange that someone as controlling as Black would take such a laid-back attitude and I wondered if he quite liked the idea of scaring me.

I had been to London on a couple of school trips but never on my own and the prospect scared me. Although I had been a precocious teenager, I had lived a totally sheltered life for some years now. As a result I was not at all streetwise, and quite vulnerable. I had no idea what to do, so in the end I asked Hugh and Olivia Porter for help. They told me to register with an employment agency in order to find a job.

I dressed in one of my church outfits, a modest navy-blue suit – the type an elderly grandmother might wear – and, without any further planning, took a train to London. When I alighted on the platform my legs were shaking with nerves but I forced myself to walk along the main road outside the station, hoping somehow an employment agency would loom into view. One did, and I felt enormous joy and relief, until I realized I had to go in. I tried to calm myself, breathed deeply and pulled the door open. To my amazement I came face to face with Bruce Keay, one of Kerry's friends, who was sitting behind a desk near the entrance.

We'd last met years ago up north and he seemed delighted to see me again. He asked what I was doing in London and I explained I needed a job. He said he would sort me out, asked me lots of questions about my qualifications and created a CV for me on the spot. He then looked through his files and suggested I try a market-research company that had offices nearby and needed someone to type documents, help with the filing and, if I was thought sufficiently reliable and intelligent, to assist in some of the quantitative research.

Bruce rang them straight away and they agreed to see me. I found their offices and was interviewed by a middle-ranking executive and a lady from HR. They asked me to take a maths test and, to my surprise and delight, I scored 100 per cent. So much for Black saying I was stupid, I thought. Although they hadn't intended to consider a school-leaver, they decided to offer the job to me. I accepted immediately and felt very proud. As the summer sales were still on I bought a couple of outfits from Dorothy Perkins and Laura Ashley that I thought would be suitable for wearing in an office.

I began working and settled into the life of a commuter. I loved earning my own money and didn't find the work too difficult but I felt uncomfortable with the other staff as I had nothing in common with them. It was a massive culture shock being with people who weren't Church members. Even so, the fact that I now had independent means and the beginnings of a life outside Tadford didn't open my eyes to the possibility of anything being different. Most of the time I found it very difficult to think for myself. Even though I worked in London I still went to Church assemblies on Monday and Wednesday evenings, Sunday morning and evening, and sometimes on Saturday night. The congregation varied between 250 and 300, and assemblies lasted over two hours and always reinforced what was expected of you.

Nonetheless July was turning out to be a good month and I was looking forward to seeing my family at the Church's summer weekend conference. They had written that they would be coming and hoped that now I had finished my education we could see more of each other.

Since they had first left me at Tadford, I was no longer the defiant, immature teenager they remembered and our relationship was bound to be different. I was, of course, pleased to see Mum and Dad, but our lack of regular and intimate contact made me feel very distant from them. I couldn't relax with them for a moment. Nor did happy memories of family life come flooding back. Instead, I found it all very awkward and stiff, and didn't have much to say. I did, though, ask Dad if in principle he thought it would be a good idea for me to go to university. It was a pointless question because I knew Black didn't want me to, but I felt very pleased when he said that he approved and he thought I would do well.

We didn't spend much time together during my parents' visit. I and the other young women in the Church were sleeping together in the Church schoolrooms so that we were on hand to help with the conference. About three hundred people came and there was lots to do, from preparing and serving the meals to cleaning the toilets.

Conferences were ideal occasions to encourage people to join the Church, but Black didn't want just anybody. Some visitors were hand-picked from around the country and invited personally. Others who just turned up would be questioned and quietly scrutinized. Those the Church leaders thought would add something to the Church, either financially or because they had a talent – and this could range from being a musician to being an electrician – would be made to feel very special. Black would try to talk to each person about his or her skills and intimate that whatever they were could be put to better use in the Church. He would invite them to his home for dinner where he'd talk about spiritual growth and how they were coming to the place where God dwelt. For the selected visitors special treatment would extend to free accommodation and the food they were given. When a barbecue was prepared, they would be given top-quality lamb chops while regular Church members often had to make do with chicken legs.

My Scottish friend Rob Jarvis, who was a wonderful handyman, was given the full treatment and he, his wife Moira and three small children were slowly reeled in like a prize catch. They were told Tadford was a wonderful place, that the children were beautiful and, unlike other kids, didn't take drugs, drink or smoke, and that it would be an oasis for the family in an increasingly cynical world.

There was another reason why I didn't spend much time with my parents. I had a more pressing issue on my mind and it was Peter Jones. Peter and I had been friendly since I stayed with his aunt and uncle when I was much younger, but at this conference we suddenly hit it off and talked and laughed throughout. Peter, no longer a teenager, was tall, blond and handsome, with straight teeth and a powerful physique. He worked as a fitness coach and told me he loved seeing the people under his charge be transformed from overweight and unfit 'lumps' (his word!) to being – if not Olympic world-beaters – then at least people who had gained a new-found respect for their bodies.

I liked him but I knew full well that no one was allowed a boyfriend at Tadford. If you went out with someone you married him. There was no casual dating. Nor was there much choice as you weren't allowed to look outside of the Church for a boyfriend or marry someone who wasn't a member. Black used to say we weren't allowed to be 'asymmetrically paired', which meant we weren't allowed to marry someone who hadn't been saved – that is, anyone who didn't attend Tadford. By now I was so indoctrinated and assimilated that I felt that if Black wanted me to find someone from within the Church to marry then that is what I must do.

After the conference I kept thinking about Peter and did my best to accidentally on purpose bump into him. I was delighted when we began to hang around together after assembly for a chat. It must have been obvious that there was something between us because after a couple of weeks Black began to smile knowingly at me and I took his reaction as a definite sign that he approved.

Around this time I also had a long chat about marriage with Black's elder daughter, Ione, who told me her father had said that the only answer to my rebellious ways was to get married. I didn't pick up at the time that Black was also working behind the scenes and had almost certainly spoken to Peter's aunt and guardian, Celia, about what was happening between Peter and me, and had indicated that he was in favour of the relationship. As founders of the Church, Celia and her husband Patrick were so embedded in its ways that they would never have contemplated anything that Black disapproved of – and certainly not the marriage of their nephew, whose well-being had been placed into their trust. Black also kept saying 'well done' to Peter, which Peter assumed referred to me. I believe he wanted me to get married to keep me at the Church.

Towards the end of August events took a giant leap forward when Peter asked if I would come out to dinner with him, his aunt and his cousin Carol. I immediately realized the importance of the invitation. He wanted to marry me. All dating couples had to have a chaperone, so the date had obviously been sanctioned by his aunt and uncle, and Black himself. The venue was a local curry house – at that time my favourite food – where you could eat as much as you wanted from the buffet for £5 per head. My excitement at such a significant event didn't dampen my appetite and I chose a bit of everything: chicken korma, chicken tikka masala and lamb balti. I followed the main course with a pistachio-flavoured kulfi and washed everything down with lashings of Coca-Cola. Peter chose hotter dishes that I couldn't touch, as I'd once had a bad experience with a vindaloo. His uncle didn't come because he was working, but it was a very relaxed evening because I knew Celia and Carol so well.

When it was time to go home Peter gave me a peck on the cheek, which I knew was also extremely significant. The next day all my friends, as well as other members of the Church, knew about our meal together.

It wasn't surprising. Tadford was such a small, closed community and almost everyone thrived on gossip, especially if it was about relationships.

My eighteenth birthday followed a week later. I still wasn't allowed to travel home to see my parents, so instead they organized a small family celebration in Southampton, where Kerry was doing her doctorate. I wore a modest Laura Ashley dress and even though I had seen my parents just a few weeks previously, I continued to find them hard to communicate with. From an outsider's point of view, it was obviously the ideal opportunity to tell them about the terrible restrictions I'd had to endure and ask them to help me escape. But I was far too brainwashed to even think along those lines. Countless times I had listened to Black say how families held you back and that it wasn't God's way to associate with people who were not true Christians, by which he meant those people who weren't members of the Church, and I believed it. As a result I felt very distant, and thought the conversation was so stilted and not nearly Christian enough that I was pleased to get back to Tadford, where I could be more at ease.

Peter and I could only go out together if we were chaperoned by his aunt or if we were in a large group of other young people, and our dates were mainly spent chatting and drinking tea. A few weeks later, a day I'll never forget, Peter and I were at his aunt and uncle's house watching a documentary about polar bears. I hadn't seen his aunt and thought we were on our own for the first time. We sat close together on the sofa holding hands under a blanket, and suddenly, just before the documentary ended, he asked me to marry him. I said, 'Pardon me. What did you say?' He asked me again and I replied, 'Yes. OK.' And that was that. I went to kiss him and he came towards me. I wanted a passionate kiss like I had experienced when I was a young teenager. He tried to give me a peck on the cheek. I laughed, half in embarrassment, and said, 'You have never kissed a girl before, have you?' 'No,' he said. I was his first girlfriend and I had to show him what to do.

After just the one brief kiss he said he wanted to tell his aunt the news. She had been hiding somewhere in the house, waiting to hear. She came in and said she was very pleased for us and that I was the answer to her prayers. I then went home to phone Mum and Dad. They were shocked. I had only left school in July. I hadn't mentioned anything about Peter during my birthday dinner and here I was already engaged. Dad said he thought it was a bit sudden and asked if I was doing the right thing. I thought it was a strange comment. Why didn't he instantly grasp that Ian Black had given us his blessing, which meant it was God's will that Peter and I were together? The fact that we had been going out together for only a few weeks was totally irrelevant. I wasn't rude, but firmly told him it was The Right Thing To Do. Mum was delighted and said it was wonderful news, and that she liked Peter and his aunt and uncle very much.

I was pleased, although I didn't know if I actually loved him. I had no idea what being in love actually felt like. It was far more important to do what Black expected of me. I knew that 18 was the age at which the Church liked girls to marry and it was normally a time of enormous pressure. If you didn't find someone you really liked you either had to compromise and marry someone you didn't mind or not get married at all. I knew of several really nice girls who had been 'left on the shelf' – ridiculous though this phrase sounds to me today when applied to women of such a young age – and I felt huge relief that I wasn't going to be one of them. Arguing about a possible career was brave enough, but as far as marriage was concerned it was out of the question to take the wrong path.

Celia threw an engagement party for us two weeks later. We had about sixty guests, but it didn't occur to me for a second to invite my own parents or my sister. I'd been keen to tell them my news, but they no longer seemed relevant to my future life. I bought a new dress in red and velvet and we had a large cake with lavender icing with my and Peter's names written across it. All the guests clubbed together to buy us a set of

French cast-iron saucepans that were all the rage at the time.

Black popped into the party but didn't stay long. A few days later Kerry came to see me. She wanted to take me out for lunch and show off her first car, a Triumph Herald, but I wasn't allowed out with her by myself, so it was a wasted journey. I didn't mind. I was too full of being engaged and preparing for my wedding. During the hour that I was allowed to see her, Kerry asked me a few odd questions about how the Church was treating me, but as she was now the only member of the family who wasn't a Christian I felt embarrassed by her presence and didn't take any notice or pick up on what might have been heavy hints. I had no idea that she was so worried about the encompassing influence Tadford was having on me that she was building up a dossier with the aim of kidnapping me from a Church she now believed had several of the marks of a cult. She had talked about it with a group of friends who were keen to help her but in the end she didn't go through with it because she believed I wouldn't come with her. She was right. Now I was engaged my life in the Church took on a whole new meaning and Tadford was where I belonged for good.

Once Peter and I were engaged we started looking for a house. As Church members we were required to live very close to Tadford, so our choice was restricted. We eventually found a tiny two-bedroom former council house on a nearby estate. It cost £29,000, which seemed an enormous amount at the time, and Peter put down a fairly hefty deposit. We completed the purchase of the property about six weeks before we got married, although it was out of the question for us to move in together.

The date for our wedding was fixed for the following spring and there was masses to do. I decided to start with the best bit, picking my wedding dress. It was something that, like most women, I had secretly been looking forward to from the time I was a young girl. Mum wasn't around, so I asked Peter's cousin Carol, who was a good friend, to help me. We chose a Thursday so we could go late-night shopping in London and we both felt very excited. My first stop was a bridal specialist, where I felt like a princess as I tried on one dress after another. It was such an exciting thing to do. After I had tried on about six dresses I picked out one that had a tight bodice and was made of white taffeta. Once it was on I fell completely in love with it. Carol loved it too. It cost £200 and I decided I just had to have it. I also chose two pale-pink bridesmaids' dresses, which luckily were reduced in price. I paid for these and put a deposit on the wedding dress.

I felt I'd just had the best time of my life and got home bubbling over with excitement. I couldn't wait to go round to tell Celia that I had put a deposit on my dress and how beautiful it was. That night I barely slept, I was so excited.

But my excitement was short-lived as I had forgotten one of the fundamental rules of Tadford. Individuals didn't make personal choices, even when it came to one of the most important and exciting personal decisions of one's life, choosing the date of your wedding. When I arrived home from work the next day I was called to Black's office and told in his inimitable way that I was not allowed to decide when my wedding would take place without asking and that instead he would decide when the 'happy day' would be. It was an extraordinary piece of micro-management for a world-travelling Church leader, but typical of a man I considered to be a control freak. I tried to argue with him, but he wouldn't budge. I was devastated.

As usual I had to help out at the Christmas conference and this time Kerry turned up. I again felt very embarrassed by her presence, especially when she said she had come only to see me and refused to go to any of the services. I knew it would be obvious to everyone that she wasn't a Christian. She did, though, join in with the communal lunch. It was a disaster. Black strode up to her and, without any preliminaries, repeated what was almost becoming a mantra, that unless she became a committed Christian she would go to Hell. He then strode off to talk to someone else. Although I felt Kerry was wrong not to become a Christian, he had no reason to behave in that way. After all she was doing a doctorate, was perfectly respectable and had arrived dressed modestly. I was pleased when she left as I didn't want to feel an emotional pull towards my family.

I didn't see my parents over Christmas but once the festivities were over I decided to go and see them. Black was not at all happy to hear where I was going and insisted that Peter come with me. I suppose he didn't trust me to go by myself in case I decided not to come back. But he trusted Peter. We left on a Friday evening after work, with Peter driving, and it took us five hours to get up north. It felt very strange going home for the first time since I was a young teenager. My life had changed so much that when we finally arrived I felt no emotion. Home no longer felt like home. I was much more interested in looking towards the future and my life with Peter.

My parents had made up beds in separate bedrooms. Peter was put in the guest bedroom while I slept in my original bed in my old room, which felt very weird. My parents hadn't changed it much but I noticed that the discharged cartridges from the clay-pigeon shooting had gone. There was no hanky-panky between Peter and me, but I did manage to sneak into his room for a very well-behaved cuddle first thing in the morning. After breakfast Mum took me to shopping, leaving Peter behind at home with Dad. While we were in the town's only department store, Mum told me that that she and Dad liked Peter very much and thought we would have a marvellous Christian marriage. She didn't even mind when I told her that, unlike most brides' mothers, she wouldn't be involved in any of the planning as that would be done by Peter's aunt and uncle because they were members of the Church. She said she was hopeless at that sort of thing anyway and was quite happy just to share the wedding costs with Celia and Patrick. Dad later added that he was thrilled I had found a really nice lad and was marrying into a lovely family. If they noticed any change in me and worried that I was much more withdrawn and uncommunicative than the daughter they knew, they were tactful enough to not say anything. Perhaps they put it down to the fact that I was tired from the drive and generally tense about the wedding.

In the afternoon I went to see Debbie, who had been a very good school friend. She seemed really pleased to see me and put on a record by the Human League as we sat down to talk in her front room. I wasn't up to speed on the Human League – or indeed on any other pop group she tried to talk about – and felt that I had arrived from another planet. There was no connection between us and we spent a very uncomfortable hour or so together.

Fortunately my parents were lovely and supportive. They brought out the family albums and we enjoyed showing Peter the photographs. We also went for walks with their new King Charles spaniel, Duke, which helped lighten the atmosphere. Naturally we also talked about the wedding.

In one way I quite enjoyed myself but it felt so strange being home with my parents that I couldn't fully relax. I kept feeling I should be at Tadford. At least there I knew exactly what was expected of me, what I should think, how I should be and even what I should wear. At the time I didn't realize that this was indicative of how much my mind had become programmed and controlled. Peter, on the other hand, seemed relaxed and happy to be quiet, partly, I think, because he was exhausted from the journey. I was relieved when we could leave on Sunday morning. Peter and I chatted throughout the journey, planning our future life together, and I told him I wanted only two children as I didn't think I could manage more than that.

Once the invitations had been posted announcing our wedding on the day that Black had chosen, Dad's joy at my forthcoming nuptials took a serious knock. He and Mum had planned to bring down a busload of friends from Bethesda Charismatic Church to the wedding, but when they mentioned it to Pastor Collins he said he didn't want any of his parishioners to attend. He had apparently cut his ties with Black after accusing him of creaming off nearly all the key, hard-working members of his small congregation, plus half his entire membership. The result was that the little church he had built up from scratch was bleeding to death. He couldn't afford to lose anyone else to Tadford and had stopped Black coming to preach. In the end just three of my parents' friends from Bethesda travelled down to help us celebrate.

I was summoned to Black's office shortly after Peter and I returned home. This time he wanted me to bring him up to date with details about the wedding and we discussed bridesmaids, the veil and the wedding rings. For a busy man with an ever-increasing flock, it seemed extraordinary that such minute details should not just interest him but also occupy his time and energy. We locked horns straight away. I wanted Kerry and Ellen, a friend from Tadford, to be my bridesmaids, but Black refused point-blank to allow Kerry to be one, as he said that she was damned. I also said that I wanted to walk up the aisle with my father to the wedding march from Wagner's *Lohengrin*, which I had always loved, but Black insisted that it be a more solemn piece by Bach.

We argued back and forth for what seemed like hours. Eventually I gave in over the bridesmaids and agreed to his choice of Peter's cousin Carol, although I was allowed to keep Ellen as one. But I stuck to my guns over the wedding march. This sort of detail is very special for a bride-to-be and in the end I got my way. It was a tiny triumph and one I am sure Black noted for the future. I don't know who called Mum to tell her about Kerry, but I couldn't face doing it. Kerry was terribly upset at the news. I was sad for her too, but I couldn't do anything about it.

A month or so before the wedding Black gave Peter and me a book on sex in marriage that outlined what a good Christian can and can't do. We both read every page. I knew Peter was a virgin, but I didn't know if he was worried about the wedding night. I also assumed he knew I wasn't a virgin. He never mentioned it, but Black hadn't kept that part of my life secret and everyone seemed to know how I had behaved before I joined the church.

Next on my to-do list was organizing my hen night. I decided on a small, intimate evening at home with Siobhan and a few girls I was reasonably friendly with. Because her flat was small I sent out invitations to just five or six friends. Two days later, after the invitations had been received, I was yet again summoned to see Black. He was angry that I had invited so few people and told me he wanted every woman in the church involved in my hen party and suggested a night at the local hotel instead. It was the opposite of what I had wanted, but in the end I duly obeyed. As the whole event had been taken over I completely lost interest.

Worse was to follow. On Wednesday, four days before the wedding, Peter insisted on driving me back to Alex and Siobhan's house after church. He parked outside, then told me that his aunt had said that I wasn't good enough for him and so he was calling the wedding off. I knew his aunt had a significant influence over him, but I couldn't believe that this extended to something so major. After we entered their house, we had a mighty row in the kitchen during which I asked him why she didn't want us to marry. He didn't give me a reason and refused to criticize her in any way or even disagree with what she had cruelly said about me. I was dreadfully upset and ran into the living room crying. Siobhan asked me what was wrong, and when I told her she immediately rang Olivia Porter. They spoke and Olivia rang back about half an hour later to speak to me. She said that Black had spoken to Celia and told her she was in the wrong, that everything was fine and that the wedding could go ahead. Apparently, she was informed that Black wanted us to marry and she knew that that meant God wanted it too and immediately withdrew her objection. When I saw Peter the next day, neither of us mentioned what had happened but I never forgot what Celia really thought about me.

Chapter 6

Teenage Marriage

My marriage on that Saturday in spring took place on an overcast day with frequent squally showers. I hadn't quite recovered from the trauma of what had happened at Celia's house and felt very nervous so, just before the wedding, I had a secret glass of sherry to calm me. I also had a banana because it was easy to eat and didn't make crumbs.

The ceremony began at 2.30 p.m. in the church hall. I walked down the aisle on my father's arm, clutching my simple bouquet of pink and white flowers, to Wagner's lovely wedding march. I was followed by my brides-maids. Peter wore a morning coat with a red carnation in his lapel, a white shirt and a red polka-dot tie, and I thought he looked very handsome. Black officiated.

Mum had bought a yellow dress and jacket and a white hat with a veil, and sported a white-rose corsage.

She seemed happy, but I could tell that Kerry wasn't. Not being my bridesmaid spoilt the whole event for her. For her sister's wedding she wanted to be in a bridesmaid's dress, not the green floral dress and white hat she chose instead. She came with her husband, Neil, and believed that not only had she been prevented from being my bridesmaid but that Black didn't want her there at all. She didn't tell me until years later that she was also convinced that she would lose me for ever once I married within the Church. We were all pleased, though, that Roy came and behaved perfectly. I also felt relieved that Celia seemed to have put her doubts about me behind her and behaved like a genuinely happy aunt and guardian of the groom.

During the wedding service Black repeatedly told me that I had to obey my husband. Otherwise I can't remember much about it. After the ceremony we took over a local hotel for the reception. We had 120 guests. Our buffet consisted of salmon mousse, chicken and various salads, with Waldorf pudding for dessert. I was too nervous to eat and just nibbled pieces of chocolate that were on our table. We had a traditional three-tier wedding cake edged with pink to match the bridesmaids' dresses. There was no alcohol and no dancing but my Dad, the best man and Peter all gave speeches, though I was so tense that I can't remember any of them.

After a couple of hours I changed into a sober dark suit and matching hat. Peter and I then got into the rented white Austin Allegro that my parents had laid on for us. Everyone threw confetti and squirted us with foam. I was sorry to go so early as I hadn't seen my relatives for many years and would have loved to chat longer to them and to my sister Kerry. My wedding should have been the best day of my life but mine didn't feel like that. I couldn't help thinking about all the arguments I'd had over the date of my wedding, the bridesmaids and the wedding march, and what Celia really thought of me. Marrying Peter was what Black expected from me, so I rationalized, as Celia had done, that it must also be what God wanted me to do.

We chose Blackpool for our honeymoon destination. It didn't sound very glamorous but a friend of Peter's from work knew someone who ran a hotel there and said it was a cheap place to stay. We decided to try it and booked a room with a view of the sea.

Once I was actually married, my feelings of tension melted away and I looked forward to our being Mr and Mrs Jones. Unfortunately the moment we arrived in Blackpool after a long drive Peter said that he felt ill. We managed to consummate the marriage in between bouts of his being sick but as the evening progressed he became so feverish that I let him have the double bed to himself and moved into the single bed. He went on vomiting for three days and was so poorly with the bug that he had picked up, widely known today as winter vomiting disease, that he couldn't leave the room and certainly didn't want any food. I stayed with him most of the time but occasionally took a break to get something to eat or wander around Blackpool. It was hardly enjoyable on my own.

At the end of the third day he still felt so dreadful that we decided to come home early. I had just learnt to drive, and although I had only passed my driving test a month earlier and was unaccustomed to motorways, I drove the whole way back. It was a terrible trip because he kept stopping to throw up. With hindsight we should have called a doctor, but for some reason it didn't occur to either of us. It shows how naive we were.

We moved into our tiny two-bedroom house and I was thrilled to see all our presents piled up in the little sitting room. We had filled the house with furniture from my grandmother's home. Her husband had recently died and this had made her decide that she could no longer cope in such a large house so she was moving to a small bungalow and told us to take what we wanted. We didn't mind that some of it was rather old-fashioned. Black didn't want us to have a television because he said there was a lot of evil in the world and we could not be trusted to watch suitable programmes. He admitted that he had a television but only because he was mentally strong enough to cope with whatever he saw. It would take me a while to realize that there were many inconsistencies between Black's teaching and his own conduct and practices.

Our honeymoon had been a disaster but it was exciting to open all our presents and much more so to have our own home. I felt very lucky. At first living together felt a bit like playing mummies and daddies without the children, and I enjoyed commuting to and from work. Unfortunately my first job at the market-research firm had only lasted a month. The directors of the firm asked me to leave after deciding that, despite my obvious mathematical proficiency, I wasn't experienced enough to cope with the work. I came home in tears feeling it was all my fault, and when I told Black he said I was obviously lazy and must go straight back to the employment agency and get another job. Fortunately the company had given me an excellent reference because they believed it was their error in employing an inexperienced school-leaver. I found more work very easily, as a secretary at a quantity surveyors. I enjoyed my work greatly but must have irritated my colleagues by criticizing them when they swore and telling them God would punish them if they didn't go to church.

At home I did all the cooking, but I wasn't very good and we had a few disasters. My first roast I lovingly put into the oven and when we came to eat it an hour or so later I realized it was still raw because I hadn't switched the oven on. To my relief, Peter just laughed. I hadn't improved much by our first Christmas together. We wanted to have a romantic Christmas dinner on our own, so, as a change from what we normally had, I bought a frozen goose from the local supermarket. I hadn't cooked a goose before and assumed that its rather odd smell was normal. Unfortunately it smelt even worse after it was cooked. I told Peter I didn't think we should eat it and we gave it to our cat instead. The poor thing spent all Christmas vomiting over the lawn. Luckily Peter's aunt and uncle lived close by and we knew we'd eat well there as Celia was a brilliant cook. It hadn't crossed my mind to spend Christmas with my parents up north or invite them to join us, but I did send presents and cards.

A few months after our wedding Kerry came to a conference at Tadford. She had been growing increasingly worried both about me being in such an inward-looking organization before I'd had a chance to experience real life, and about the growing distance between me and the family. The way she was treated merely added to her fears. Apparently she was taken to one side by one of the senior Church members and told, like all of us had been, that she was full of evil and that if she didn't stay at Tadford she would be doomed. It's something that can only be described as repellent, but was obviously a proven way to recruit members. She was also told to give up her doctorate in occupational therapy and all of her friends. On the surface she remained immune to the alarmist threats that tried to put the fear of God into her, but later she told me that she still felt very nervous driving home, just in case they were right.

Kerry even argued with our parents about me being at Tadford but instead of listening they were angry with her and, almost quoting Black's words, told her she was full of sin. It's probably difficult to understand how parents could behave so badly, but my mother, in particular, had been totally taken in by the unforgiving message of fundamentalism and at the time genuinely believed that anyone who wasn't a Christian would go to Hell. I know her motive was to try to save her daughter. This strong difference of opinion caused a rift in their relationship for a couple of years but fortunately they were then reconciled.

Although Peter and I were both earning quite well, money was still tight. This was because we had to give so much to the Church. Black regularly preached that Church members were obliged to give 10 per cent of their gross salary to the Church as a tithe. It was a substantial amount, especially as the Church, which was a registered charity, could also claim the tax back. Black gave the impression that making these donations was the least we could do because all money belonged to God in the first place.

In addition to the tithes, there were regular requests for money for things the Church needed. In common with many Charismatic Churches, these were known as 'altar calls' at Tadford. Black would get everyone to stand up and pledge what they could. Sometimes it would be asked for in the form of paper money, cheques of a minimum of £5 or written pledges. At other times the amount requested started as high as £20,000 and gradually went down in set amounts to £100. Once an individual had pledged an amount, he or she sat down. It meant that those left standing felt pressured and humiliated into making a pledge. In this way very large sums of money, in addition to the regular tithes, could be raised in a single meeting. The atmosphere was always charged and it was all very public, so everyone knew who was and who was not giving generously. Some people who had no spare money would even remortgage their home or sell possessions to be able to donate to the Church. I know of others who got into such financial difficulties that they asked Black if they could work outside the Church to earn a salary rather than work for nothing for the Church, but their requests were nearly always turned down.

Members were encouraged to give generously and told by Black that God would reward them 'many times over'.

Fear also played a large part. We, like other members of the Church, dared not go against Black and believed if we did we would die a terrible premature death. In addition to all these financial pressures, we also had to give £50 a month towards the running of the school, even though we didn't yet have any children.

For most of the time, though, life felt good and I was happy. It felt special making a home together with Peter, gathering and arranging our furniture, deciding on what we wanted to eat and when. We loved inviting other members of the Church round to our home to chat, but we always kept Sunday night as a special time for the two of us. I had learnt how to make Eccles cakes and we would turn the electric lights off and eat them under the light of candles. We used to joke that we should have been born in an earlier century because we liked old-fashioned things.

We also enjoyed silly childish banter and going for walks together. We both loved the countryside, and I would pack a flask of hot chocolate and take some biscuits with us. We talked about having a family and what it might be like being parents. Peter agreed with me that two children were quite enough.

He took me out for romantic meals and I thought he was very sweet. His gentleness, combined with his well-developed physique, appealed to me greatly. He also loved fashioning home-made fishing rods and his own lures, but although we often used to go and try these out on nearby rivers and ponds, we rarely caught anything.

Despite our closeness Peter made it clear right from the start that the Church always had to come first, which indicated I would come second. It meant that as soon as he had eaten his dinner after work he'd go to help out there. He did an enormous range of jobs, from anything to do with plumbing to working on recordings of the Church conferences. I accepted this and knew how important the Church would always be in our lives. The one thing I did find distressing was that he worked so hard for both us and the Church that when he was at home he would often get terrible stomach cramps – later diagnosed as IBS – that would keep him in bed for sometimes as long as two days.

Time passed quickly and just over a year after our wedding, we set off to Germany, where Tadford was holding a week-long conference. These conferences had originally started in England and had by now developed into something grander and more prestigious, and were often held overseas. People would come from all over Europe and further afield, and there would often be guest speakers. On this occasion the Church had booked a large conference centre in a small town north of Frankfurt and about two hundred of us attended. We went to prayer meetings, ate good food, did some sight-seeing and generally enjoyed ourselves. I remember one night in particular when Peter and I set off a couple of fire extinguishers in the hostel where the majority of us were staying, drenching a number of people. We thought our jape was hilarious, but really it showed that we were both still children.

By the end of the week I realized I hadn't had my period, which was unusual as I was very regular. I also began to feel sick. When we got married I started taking a regular contraceptive pill, but after a few months the doctor changed it to a Progesterone-only pill. When I was 18 it was discovered that I had a blood clot in my leg and so he recommended the mini-pill instead, which although not quite as reliable was less dangerous.

When I got home I took a urine sample to the doctor and it came back positive. I was totally shocked, and I felt far too young and immature to have a child. I had assumed I would be safe with the mini-pill but I know there can be problems if you don't take the pill at the same time every day, and perhaps I had slipped up. My anxiety soon gave way to excitement. It is always a blessing to be able to have a child and Peter, who was just as pleased, and I started planning for our new future. The financial implications were going to be tricky. We were only just about managing on both our salaries and I knew that I wouldn't be able to work in the same way once we had a baby.

Once my pregnancy was confirmed I resigned from my job at the quantity surveyors as I didn't feel up to the daily commute to London and instead took a job as a cashier in the local pizza parlour. It was long before the law banning smoking in restaurants came into effect and many of the customers smoked heavily both before and after their meal. The smoky atmosphere made me sick and I gave up work entirely when I was six months' pregnant.

Once we had to live without my salary Peter felt his wage wouldn't be enough for us to live on. He had recently taken a TEFL course in his spare time, hoping that working in this field would supplement his meagre income as a fitness coach. At this time many foreign students were coming to England to learn English and he found a position in a language college that, if not brilliantly paid, certainly helped us make ends meet.

Meanwhile I had started nesting in a big way and the closer the birth, the more excited I felt. I made all my maternity clothes and little sheets for the baby from one big flannelette sheet. Celia and Patrick bought us a cot and Mum and Dad, who were very excited about me giving birth, gave me a lovely oak changing table and dresser.

I went to antenatal classes and Peter came to the fathers' night, but we didn't mix with any of the couples because they were not Church members, and I didn't see them after we had our babies. The pregnancy changed things between us. I needed Peter to be with me and I worried, like many first-time mums, about how I would cope and the responsibility of being a young mother. Peter's life, however, hadn't changed at all and he continued to leave me on my own most evenings to work for the Church. I felt working for nothing for the Church ate into the time and energy he could give to his language teaching or spend with me. But he felt he was doing God's work and was angry that I was trying to pull him away from his calling. I was unhappy that his commitment seemed to be to the Church rather than to me. We had a massive argument when I was eight months' pregnant. I was complaining that he seemed more committed to the Church than to me, when he suddenly exploded with incandescent rage. It came as such a shock I thought I might go into early labour at any minute. I think he realized he had gone too far and apologized when things calmed down. I felt he genuinely meant it and accepted his apology. Looking back, I realize how needy and immature I was, and that when we had an argument I would go on and on and on without knowing when to stop.

Paul was born the following month, weighing 8 lb 8 oz, after a straightforward labour. Peter was with me but from start to finish was almost frozen to the spot with fear. I felt very weak afterwards but I thought Paul was absolutely beautiful, a perfect little doll. Peter was equally thrilled with him, as were his aunt and uncle. I stayed in the hospital for five days because Paul had a respiratory infection and had to be treated with intravenous antibiotics. My parents came soon after to meet him, which I was very pleased about, and Mum stayed for a few weeks to help me.

Midwives were very strict with new mothers in those days and mine insisted that I spend the first ten days at home and not go out. When she gave me the all-clear my first outing was to buy a new dress to wear for Church. I was so looking forward to showing Paul off to the congregation but I hadn't realized what a palaver it was to go anywhere with a new baby. We decided to give Paul his first experience of church on a Sunday. When we got there, I went into the mums' room next to the recording room to feed him, but he was sick all over me and my new dress, and Peter had to take me straight home.

The first month or two after Paul's birth passed in a blur. Initially I found looking after him rather daunting, but gradually I got the hang of it and before long started having coffee mornings for other young mothers at home and going on trips to the nearby shopping centre.

Peter behaved like a typical man, wondering what I had done all day and not realizing how time-consuming it was to look after a baby. His routine barely changed. He carried on going to work, coming home, eating his dinner, taking the occasional language class and then going to do jobs for the Church. At that time they were building new changing rooms for the school and he was very involved in sorting out the plumbing, but he was never paid a penny for his work. Luckily I was completely fulfilled being a mother. I felt so maternal, and breast-fed Paul until he was a year old. It was a very special part of being a woman and a real privilege. It was just as well I did. Black used to hold regular parents' meetings to tell us what to do with our children and expected every mother to breast-feed. Anyone who didn't, for whatever reason, was made to feel very guilty.

When Paul was about six months old we moved home. We sold our two-bedroom house for almost double what we had paid for it, and moved to a larger house with a long garden in a newly built estate nearby. We quickly settled in and found we had wonderful neighbours called Dinah and Trevor Morris, with whom we gradually became close friends. They were not churchgoers and in the controlled world in which Peter and I lived, where everything we did and everyone we spoke to seemed to be known, our friendship was frowned upon. Black didn't actually interfere, but Peter's aunt told us she thought the friendship was unhealthy because they were not Church members. Sometimes I felt I was surrounded by spies. Anything that happened in the home or with friends got straight back to Black and his cronies.

I think Mum hoped that once I became a mother we would get closer and she would play a more important part in my life. Instead Kerry's prediction was right and I grew more distant from the whole family. Phone calls were rare and their visits became even rarer. But Mum did come to Tadford for my birthday and I noticed she had a long talk with Black. I didn't think much about it as I was rather preoccupied with Paul. I was totally astonished when, completely out of the blue, she suddenly turned up on my doorstep a week or so later with a vast suitcase, saying she had come to stay for good. Peter looked thunderstruck and I felt hugely embarrassed. Black kept repeating that my parents were a bad influence on me. It was his way of minimizing their importance and keeping me dependent on the Church. The fact that they belonged to another Church made no difference, as, in his eyes, there *was* no other Church. Peter had absorbed all this, as had I. Although I always remained cordial to my parents, he worried about any negative effects they might have on me. On this occasion he was also rather put out that my mother had turned up without any warning.

When Mum had caught her breath she told me she felt that God wanted her to be at Tadford, but Dad had refused point-blank to become a member. She had told Black about this during her previous visit and he had apparently encouraged her to come without him, effectively breaking a rock-solid union. She also thought it would be lovely to live close to me. So she waited until Dad went to London for a meeting, then, when she had packed her case, rang him to say she was leaving him. He was devastated because they had been happily married for over thirty years. Mum agreed that they had been fine together but explained she felt compelled to become part of Tadford.

After her arrival at Tadford and our initial greetings, I couldn't believe what she was telling me and immediately rang Dad to tell him she was safe with me. He answered calmly and said he had an overwhelming feeling that everything would be all right. I later discovered that he was convinced that Mum had been manipulated by Black, who was not only still trying to increase his congregation, but seemed to have no qualms about splitting families in order to do so.

Following our conversation, Dad rang the office at Tadford and warned whoever it was that answered the phone that unless his wife came back to him he would ring the local press and get every newspaper up there to challenge Black over what had happened.

I didn't tell Mum about my discussion with Dad. Nor did she tell me that she had made an appointment to see Black the following morning. She was completely in his thrall and hoped she would be formally welcomed into the Church. Instead she returned shortly afterwards looking ashen. Troy Tyson, the Canadian evangelist, was visiting at the time and Black had torn her to pieces in front of him. In a booming voice he referred to the Bible, saying she must not leave her husband unless there had been infidelity and that if she did she would go to Hell. As she left she turned in terror to Tyson and asked for help to avoid this ghastly fate. He said that Jesus was keen on repentance. It was a small relief for her because Black had given her the impression that she had no hope at all.

Peter and I were then called to see Black, who told us my mother was going home. We were offered no other information. Peter took her to the station. I felt sad about sending her off when she was obviously in considerable distress, but Peter was so angry that I dared not argue with him. Luckily Dad met her at the other end, lovingly, and gently took her home, and they quickly settled back together again. Kerry thought Mum's behaviour in delivering herself to the Church was because she was gullible and needy, and that she had been through so much with Roy that she was looking for someone to tell her what to do.

Gradually I began to notice that Black had a habit of getting involved with one individual in a marriage while the other, for whatever reason, was first partly and then completely ostracized. He did something similar to another Tadford member some years later. A woman called Anna later told me that Black had informed her that her husband, Graham, whom she married in the mid-sixties, would never succeed in life because he wasn't a Tadford Christian and that she should join the Church without him. Black went on to accuse the man of being twisted, corrupt and perverse, and being a photographer for girly mags. He produced no evidence for any of these charges and the so-called pornographic photographs turned out to be images that had been used to illustrate skin complaints in a medical journal. He even accused Graham of sexually abusing a young girl, an allegation that was later withdrawn following legal letters from Graham's solicitor. The poor man was devastated by the accusations and that his wife, with whom he was deeply in love, ostracized him when she joined the Church.

When Paul was about eighteen months old he started at the Church's crèche. By this time Tadford School had a crèche, playschool, and infant and junior sections, as well as a senior school with a sixth form for A Level pupils. Paul settled in reasonably well but the staff told me they were a little concerned that he wasn't communicating as well as the other children. It didn't worry me. The health visitor wasn't concerned about him and to me he just seemed a quiet child.

By now I was by pregnant again and also helping out with the toddler group. All parents who used the school were expected to work there voluntarily despite the fact that we were already paying school fees. I worked with children aged between eighteen months and three years for many years after my next three children were born. I didn't have any child-care qualifications and my duties included helping the children with painting and gluing, potty-training them and lending a hand with the meals.

The nursery was housed in a two-roomed annexe that had been built onto one side of the converted warehouse. All the babies' cots were in a brightly painted room, while the toddlers and pre-school children were in the other.

Lunch was served at 12 p.m. and when it was ready one of us would go to collect it from the kitchen that had been installed in one corner of the warehouse. The children always had home-cooked meals, and lamb and chicken were particularly popular. We'd cut the meat into small pieces for the toddlers and liquidize the food for the babies.

All members of the Church, and these included solicitors, doctors, various consultants, lots of teachers and many others who were successful in their work, were told by Black that if a child had not been brought under control, which meant being obedient and God-fearing by the age of 2, it would be difficult ever to control him or her, and if the child was not under firm control by the age of 5, all was lost. He taught that love for a child should be expressed through regular chastisement while teenage rebellion was presented as the inevitable consequence of a lack of early and regular discipline. Refusing to eat all his or her food was considered the first sign of rebellion in a child and should therefore be punished from babyhood onwards.

Black taught that the best way to do this was either by force-feeding or smacking the child. In this context he would employ the phrase 'use the rod and save the child', a modification of the well-known proverb, although when recordings of his sermons were released this piece of advice was always edited out, lest it cause offence. Babies would sit in high chairs at the nursery and if they refused their food one of the teachers would squeeze their nose firmly shut so that they would open their mouth and food could be pushed in. It seemed incredibly young to be made to eat, because if babies don't want to eat they will spit their food out. I was shocked to see that if one of them did spit food out he or she was hit on the hand.

The toddlers sat at low tables and had to eat everything on their plates. Those who finished their meal went out to play while the others stayed put, sometimes for as long as forty minutes, to clear their plates. But if they took that long they would get a smack on their hand or bottom. Fortunately I didn't have to smack any of the children as I was a helper rather than a qualified teacher. I hated witnessing the smacking, but my mind had been coerced to accept everything that happened in the Church without question, so I didn't make a fuss and parked what I saw right at the back of my mind.

I saw children being smacked so often that gradually, although I wasn't aware of it at the time, it began to have less of an impact upon me. We all felt we were doing God's will and helping to bring up good Christian children. It shows how taken in I was. All the haranguing and endless lectures moulded me into someone I can no longer recognize. I have never forgiven myself and when I think about it I still feel sick to very pit of my stomach. We were all basically decent individuals behaving in an unforgivable way that was accepted by those around us. But there was one particular episode that came to haunt me and helped reignite my rebellious spirit. There was a little boy in the toddler group who regularly cried when his mummy dropped him off in the morning. It was understandable because as she worked next door in the pre-school group he could hear her voice through the partition and wanted to be with her. He would cling on to her as she tried to leave him, and when she had gone I often sat him on my lap and talked to him until he calmed down.

But one particular morning he wouldn't settle and just kept on crying. Eventually one of the teachers said she was going to deal with it. She took him to the toilet and smacked him repeatedly on his bare bottom. Not surprisingly, her smacking didn't stop his tears, so she kept on and on with her barbaric treatment of him. This went on all morning. His mother must have heard him but she didn't come in. She wouldn't have been allowed to even if she had tried as it was against the rules to interfere in something that had been sanctioned by Black. After a couple of hours the child was badly bruised. When Peter came home from work I told him how horrendous I thought it had been and that I felt like calling the police. He merely said it was the rule of the Church. Although I now went along almost without question with what the Church said in every area of my life, this time I couldn't forget what I had seen. But perhaps I shouldn't have expected anything different from Peter, who was merely being consistent. I was furious that his attitude was so black and white, and this time I decided to do something about it. I went to see the school head to complain about the little fellow's treatment. Shortly afterwards I was sent to work in an allotment that the Church used at the other side of town. I suspected it was done to get me out of the way.

Peter also felt it was his duty as a devoted Church member to smack Paul when he misbehaved and did so from nine months, an age when babies develop a certain will and also start eating solids. I did nothing to stop it and in some ways became desensitized to what was happening. This continued with our other children. I occasionally smacked them too. It is something I now barely believe possible. Sometimes when Peter punished them I would cry. I had no idea how to balance my over-powering protective, maternal instincts with the feeling that I was doing what God wanted.

On one of their rare visits my parents became aware that Paul was being smacked, but they never said a word to me. They took some snaps of him as a sweet toddler in the bath. They noticed his little bottom looked a bit sore, but it was only once they got home and had the photos developed that they realized how bad it was, and that his bottom was black and blue. Understandably, they both felt sick, particularly as they had never hit any of us. They considered going to the police but rejected the idea because of the family relationship. Later on they told me that at the time they felt, as Paul's grandparents rather than parents, powerless to do anything. To be honest I don't know what I would have done if they had said something.

Chapter 7

Traumas of a Young Mother

I gave birth to Rebecca two years after the arrival of Paul. She was a little baby at 5 lb 2 oz. Peter was happy we were having another child. He was so childlike himself and loved playing with little ones, and I was thrilled to have two children so close in age. As there was a big age gap between my sister Kerry and me, we weren't close when I was small and I didn't want that for my children.

It was hard work, but luckily our wonderful neighbours, Dinah and Trevor, were a very jolly, down-to-earth and generous middle-aged couple, and you couldn't help but warm to them. I regularly saw them, not only on our street or over the hedge between our gardens, but also down at the allotment, where I spent a lot of time. They had a large patch under cultivation there and insisted on giving us lots of their freshly grown vegetables. Trevor and I shared a love of gardening, and would talk endlessly about plants together. He also taught me how to bake bread, something I'd never managed to do before. I liked Dinah and Trevor because they were so warm. They would help out with Paul and occasionally babysit for me without ever being intrusive or telling me what to do. In a way they almost became substitute parents for me, and we grew so close that Paul would point to Dinah and say 'grandma'. Sadly Trevor died suddenly from a heart attack shortly after Rebecca was born, but I stayed close to Dinah, who saved my life when I needed her most.

When Rebecca was just nine months old I found myself pregnant again, this time with twins. It was a shock, particularly as I was on the mini-pill and still breast-feeding her. It was a difficult pregnancy and I was very sick all the way through it. I was rushed to hospital with dehydration when I was seven and a half months' pregnant, which was worrying but luckily was quickly rectified. Luke and Daniel were born on a beautiful late summer's morning, with Daniel a healthy 8 lb 7 oz and Luke weighing in at 8 lb 2 oz. I was thrilled to have two more sons, and for Paul and Rebecca to have two brothers. Both of the baby boys were very beautiful, but sadly Luke was not a healthy baby. He had a heart murmur and didn't feed well.

I had had my babies in such quick succession that I could hardly believe I was already a mother of four.

Coping with the various needs of four little ones was hard work. I was terribly deprived of sleep and didn't feel I was getting nearly enough support from Peter. We continued with our usual arguments about his spending too much time at the Church and never being at home to help me, and after a particularly massive shouting match when the twins were ten weeks old, Peter raised the possibility of my being sterilized. Neither of us wanted any more children, and he said he didn't want – for reasons he never made clear – to have a vasectomy. Confusingly, and I thought contradictorily, he said he was worried about my health as my pregnancy with the twins had been so difficult and he knew I couldn't take a full-strength birth pill.

I told him I didn't think it was a good idea. I was much too young to contemplate something so dramatic, and there were more possible complications connected with sterilization than there were with a vasectomy. I assumed he then went to speak to Black because shortly afterwards we were summoned to go out to dinner with him and Heather. An invitation to a meal with them nearly always meant you were in trouble and my stomach turned as I thought, 'Here we go again. What have I done now?'

Black took us to an Indian restaurant and we had hardly ordered our meal when he called me a rude name for expecting my husband to be at home caring for the children. He told me I should be a better wife, and have the kids in bed before Peter came home so I could open the door to him wearing a basque and nothing else. Instead, Black said the atmosphere at home was so bad it was no wonder he didn't want to be with me.

I was so shocked by Black's comments and so upset that Peter said nothing to support me that I barely said a word for the rest of the meal. Apart from his appalling choice of language, Black was being inconsistent. When he forced me confess how I had lost my virginity as a young teenager he had made me feel dirty, cheap and immoral. Now he was suddenly telling me to behave in a brazen way with Peter, and I couldn't see the difference between what he was telling me to do with Peter and how a prostitute propositions a client. I believed that sex and marriage were a joint expression of love, rather than what he seemed to be promoting: a wife crudely flaunting herself at her husband. His comments made me feel more self-conscious about how I behaved with Peter, rather than less.

If that wasn't embarrassing enough, he then brought up the subject of sterilization. I was equally upset about this because it was a private matter between Peter and me. When we got home I asked Peter why he had mentioned such a personal issue to Black. He replied that it was the right thing to do. I, on the other hand, thought it was a huge invasion of our privacy, gave

Black further opportunity to control our lives, and made it feel as if there were three of us in the marriage. Partly because of my indignant reaction to Black's impertinent intrusion into my private life, I decided not to go ahead with the sterilization and went back on the pill instead.

Ian Black's powerful presence and dominant, fiery personality didn't just hang over me. I didn't know anyone who wasn't either in awe or afraid of him and all my children were instinctively wary. Paul told me that when he was a small boy he didn't like Black, and when he saw him he would try to run away and hide. He didn't dare say anything to him or even go near him because he commanded so much respect. Even when he was older he believed that Black was everyone's contact for God – like the Messiah. Rebecca also found him intimidating and scary. She was petrified even when he said, 'Hello, Rebecca', and one of her earliest memories was hanging on tightly to my leg when he came near.

But Black was omnipresent, and endlessly hearing his views in both informal settings like restaurants and formally in church was a key part of life at Tadford. Church services, or 'assemblies' as they were more often called, occurred three or four times a week – on Monday, Wednesday and Friday evenings – the Friday meeting was dropped shortly after Peter joined Tadford – and Sunday morning and sometimes evening. If Black was in town, no one was complete without one of his sermons.

These assemblies frequently lasted over two hours. They were repetitious and rambling, and a triumph of presentation over content. Black could capture his audience and manipulate our emotions and fears with his words, but there was little intellectual – and still less spiritual – content in what he said. Although his approach to the Bible was fairly simplistic, his delivery was so magnetic that many of the congregation trembled as they believed they were hearing the voice of God.

It was extraordinary how, through sheer force of personality, he could browbeat highly educated individuals who had well-paid and successful careers so that they became timid followers who meekly complied with his will. Almost all of us were putty in his hands and came under his sway in a manner that had to be seen to be believed. He certainly would not tolerate a question from anyone in the congregation that might throw doubt on his authority. 'No one,' he declared to one visitor, 'is going to run this Church but me, because God gave me the responsibility.' To another critic he said, 'I don't care about your intellect … Have you a right to disagree? Yes, of course you have. There is the door. Vote with your feet if you don't agree.'

Black's sermons were often over the top and downright creepy, although I didn't always realize that at the time.

Many quickly became a blur and were indistinguishable from each other, but certain sermons stood out. I remember him delivering several sermons in a low, heavy, languid, almost hypnotic voice that you wouldn't normally expect to hear from a religious leader. The following words from one of his sermons are representative of his simple but unfortunately deeply effective style: 'Jesus, I adore you,' he began in a long, very deep drawl, stretching out each word. 'I surrendered to you … When I sought you and you showed yourself to me, I felt immersed in your heavenly love. All the riches of the world are as nothing compared to just a brief moment in your company. Oh Lord, I love you from the very depths of my being.'

In other sermons he liked to talk directly to God, which made us feel that he must have an exclusive connection. For example, in another sermon he said to Jesus, 'You can command me to do whatever it is you want, and I will surely obey you.' He then turned to the congregation, to make sure we knew we too had to totally surrender our will, and added, 'Those who seek to be disciples of Jesus have to sacrifice their will to Him themselves. But not only their will. Their bodies too must be vessels for His divine inspiration.'

By first revealing his intimacy with God, then demanding complete compliance from us, Black made us feel it was natural to assume that what he wanted from us was exactly what God wanted.

Yet, at the same time, he barely concealed his widespread intolerance and lack of compassion. In one of his sermons during one of the July conferences, which had been given the optimistic title 'Tadford Weekend of Signs and Wonders', he accused men of being largely to blame for failed marriages. 'Most failed marriages,' he stated, 'are the consequence of men failing to assume their proper and sanctified roles in the home. In marriage, the man's role, and that of the woman, are clearly laid down in Holy Scripture. You might feel that you can ignore these divine precepts, but if you do you are disobeying God's law, and chaos and ignominy will certainly follow.'

Sometimes his sermons were deeply disturbing. One regular theme was to tell us that we should 'be prepared to die for Christ'. Black gave several examples of people dying for their faith at the stake and I believed in this as an ideal for many years. I believed my ticket to heaven would come if I obeyed what God specifically told me to do through the man of God – whom I believed to be Ian Black. I felt fearful when I thought, 'Is this what is being asked of me?' and 'Can I do it? Is my faith strong enough?' Deep down inside me it never was, but I often tried to convince myself it could be.

Luckily I could escape some of Black's sermons by feeding Rebecca. Together with other mothers, I would go into the room where his sermons were recorded, and smuggle in sandwiches and coffee to have as we fed our babies. I'd often try to stay in there for the entire Church assembly, so I like to think that my spirit was never totally broken. Most of the other mothers were completely submissive and never questioned anything Black said. He always had a lot of women followers. He didn't seem to have much trouble in winning them over and they would then almost automatically do what he asked.

In addition he frequently made prophecies. Like everyone else, I believed his prophecies were messages from God and for several years was in awe of him. The reality, however, was that many of his prophecies turned out to be wrong. This did not cause many, if any, Church members to stop believing in him, although later on it did give me doubts.

In one sermon, for instance, Black prophesied that a terrible persecution of Christians was imminent which would affect Tadford and that members of the Church should be ready to die for Christ.

In another sermon he prophesied over a pregnant member of the Church, stating that she would have a daughter whom she should call Rebecca. He had a 50/50 chance of being right, but in fact she had a boy.

In yet another sermon he prophesied that there would be a major earthquake in the UK within the next five years. This again did not happen.

Children were expected to attend Church assemblies with their parents on Monday and Friday nights and Sunday mornings during the school holidays. Most services finished around 10.30 p.m. and, to help with babysitting, a group of us parents would take it in turns to let several children bed down in our house so that the others could attend the meeting and then pick their children up on their way home.

None of the services was child-friendly. Children were also expected to dress formally and looked like little adults. Boys had to wear a tweed jacket, black shoes (not trainers), shirt and tie, while the girls wore blazers and modest but pretty dresses. I bought Paul a tweed jacket from a local men's outfitters, but it was so expensive that when he outgrew it I tried to get the next one in a sale.

The children were also expected to be quiet during the services, even though these usually lasted so long. This was particularly difficult as they weren't allowed to bring toys, or any drawing materials, with which to occupy themselves, nor were they allowed go out to play if they were bored. In addition, there was no special Sunday School for children, as most churches have.

If any child made a noise Black would break off from whatever he was saying and often shout in front of the whole congregation: 'Take that creature out of here and sort it out.' It was assumed to be the mother's rather than the father's role to cope with a noisy child, and it was very embarrassing when Black made it obvious that he was yelling at you. It was also taken for granted that the child would be smacked so that they knew they had to behave. They would then be brought back into the church.

Religion was never made to be fun. Instead it was based on fear and centred on Black's presence. So much so that if you asked a 4- or 5-year-old who God was, he or she would point to Black. In my view they were brainwashed from a very young age. My children soon realized they had no alternative but to be silent. Rebecca said she never dared make a sound in church because she knew she would be smacked. She would just sit there bored rigid. The same was true with Luke and Daniel.

The long services were often an endurance test for adults too. The Sunday-morning service, by far the largest of the week, had a regular congregation of about four hundred, made up of about three hundred members and a hundred visitors. It was viewed as the Church's key recruiting session and specially picked, friendly 'ushers', who were basically trusted members, would approach every visitor as they arrived and ask them about their journey and how they were.

I used to call this caring and somewhat exaggerated concern 'love bombing' and it continued when visitors entered the church hall. Greeters, including Peter's uncle

Patrick, a key founder member of the Church, would talk to newcomers, invite them to dinner and point out the Church bookshop.

Ian Black published a great number of books of his own writings, which covered everyday subjects such as child-rearing and marriage, through a company named True Prayer Press. This was part of a larger company called Holy Bloom, which relied heavily on donations from the congregation and used Tadford's premises rent free. Visitors would also be given a copy of the Church maga-zine, which was mainly filled with articles by Black or about him, and which had a print run of about 60,000. They would be asked to fill in a card with all their personal details and this information was then put on a database for mass mail-outs to prospective members.

I gradually, but secretly, felt increasingly cynical about these Sunday services. We were all so smartly dressed and wholesome it looked like a scene from the film *The Stepford Wives*. Certainly if you were a visitor – and they would regularly come not just from all corners of the UK but from Europe and as far afield as India and Brazil – the church initially looked like an amazing place. A lot of thought was given to the visual impact of the services. Black would usually wear a dark suit, white shirt and tie. The choir always looked smart, the men in white shirts with navy ties and black trousers, and the women in white shirts with navy bows and long navy skirts.

There would always be huge displays of flowers, usually in pink and white, round the stage from which Black spoke. The service itself would begin with the choir singing, followed by a couple of solos. Black would then deliver one of his sermons and perform several 'miracles'.

When the service was over, back at home we would have a traditional family Sunday roast, after which the children would usually have an afternoon nap and then sometimes go back to church in the evening, where they would sit 'bored rigid' again until about 10.30 p.m.

Monday and Wednesday night assemblies would start around 8 p.m., and when the children were small I would take a pillow and a little blanket I'd knitted for each of them into the church hall so that they could lie down and go to sleep. Once they reached the age of 6, however, they no longer had that option. Instead they were expected to take notes of what they heard during the assembly and these were subsequently marked in school.

Each child had to write a minimum of two pages on each assembly, a task Paul found extremely boring. He would write the same notes over and over again, because it seemed to him – quite rightly – that Black basically always said the same thing.

At the beginning of the Wednesday service all the chairs would be cleared away and members of the congregation would sit or lie on the floor. It was a pragmatic prelude to an emotional frenzy.

Black would shout out for the salvation of various individuals. Then he would say things like: 'We are all children of God and belong as one in his family, and we should leave the past behind us' or: 'What hinders those who genuinely seek Jesus is their family ... Families have a way of blocking Jesus' message by promoting ties that are weaker than those of God's family. Why don't you join your real family for Christmas?' The whole congregation would stand up in lines, hold hands with whoever was next to them, look them in the eye and sing:

> *I am so glad I'm a part of the family of God,*
> *Washed in the fountain, cleansed by his blood,*
> *Joint heirs with Jesus as we travel along.*
> *I'm so glad I'm a part of the Family of God.*

This was Black's way of emphasizing that we didn't or shouldn't have any other family apart from people in the Church. We'd then move on to someone else, hold their hands and say the same thing. We'd have to repeat this countless times and I hated it. As the service gathered momentum many of those present would work themselves up into a fever, and sob and scream for God to save them. Others would stand in a trance-like state for more than an hour. Black meanwhile would pick out individuals and prophesy over them. He would raise and lower his voice and speak in tongues, as if he had a secret language with God. It was impossible to understand what he was saying but at some point he'd speak in English as if interpreting the tongues.

People would then rush to the front of the hall or fall to the floor crying and hysterical. It got worse over the years, but I always found it both frightening and disturbing, particularly as the hall would become very hot as the problem of ventilation was not addressed when the warehouse was converted. Not surprisingly, by the end of the service most of the congregants were sweating from the heat and exhausted.

Keeping people in a confined and hot place has long been used in religious cleansing ceremonies, but it needs to be carefully monitored. Excessive heat can make people feel weak, dizzy, confused and disorientated. The symptoms are purely a physical reaction and can have serious consequences, but some of the members – either through ignorance or wishful thinking – often interpreted them as evidence of a religious experience.

Black also had the ability of making you feel that he was speaking directly to you. He would often intimate that that he knew things about you on the basis of what

God was telling him. I regularly thought he was referring to me but it gradually dawned on me that everyone has a weakness of some kind and it was natural to latch on to what he said as being directly addressed to you.

I discovered that he sometimes cheated too as he had already heard from one of his lieutenants what an individual's weakness was before the service. Rob Jarvis, a friend and fellow member who originally lived up north, was in Black's office when Black's temporary secretary Gwyneth, who was standing in whilst Charlotte Snelling was on maternity leave, took a call from a lady who was ill. Gwyneth suggested she come to a meeting and Rob then heard Gwyneth give Black her name, when she was coming and her medical problem.

At the due date she was in the congregation and Black called her out, prayed for her and told her everything that was wrong with her. The impression he gave was that he was hearing the information from God. On this occasion it was very subtly done, but I had known him to first declare in a loud voice, 'It is not I who heals you, but I am chosen as a channel for One who can – His name is Jesus, and He works through me.' The visitor was completely enthralled by his seeming knowledge about her, although I don't know whether or not she joined the Church.

Congregants were also encouraged to confess their sins out loud and all together at the top of their voices, beginning with prescriptive sentences. Rebecca found the experience horrific. When she was older she told me that she instinctively recoiled when they yelled, 'Oh God, save me, please save me. I don't want to go to Hell.' She told me when she was a young girl she found the noise level of several hundred people screaming and lying on the floor crying for what to her seemed like hours extremely scary.

It haunted her for years until she reached her mid-teens, when she suddenly decided that the whole thing was ridiculous. She rationalized that virtually everyone present was a baptized Christian and was already saved, so they didn't have to scream at God to save them. But at the time the atmosphere made everyone feel that he or she was a terrible sinner, and that the only way to get God to listen and help us was to cry out for our salvation.

It was so intense that, if some congregants weren't already lying down, they were expected to crash to the ground if anyone, but particularly Black, touched them. Black described this as 'the onrush of the Holy Spirit'. He would leave the stage, walk around the hall, touch people's heads, say 'In Jesus' name' and they would fall over. These occasions were emotionally very highly charged and I would cuddle my little ones to soften the impact.

Protecting my children was instinctive to me and gradually, as I matured, they became the main focus of my life. Not least because the vigorous disciplinary standards Black and his cronies insisted upon in church were enforced with even greater emphasis in the school classroom. Being a mother was totally fulfilling for me. I loved talking to my children, nurturing them, and joking and laughing together. I enjoyed watching them grow, seeing how their individual characters developed, what their strengths and weaknesses were, and how different each of them was.

When Paul and Rebecca began at Tadford School it had about fifty pupils and usually not more than eight in a class. All signed-up parents were given a thick handbook about the school that set out the Church's aims. Some of these were undoubtedly, on the surface at least, impressive and idealistic. They included helping children to develop lively and inquiring minds and helping them to question, argue rationally and apply themselves to tasks. The teachers were keen that each child should reach his or her full potential – mentally, physically, emotionally and spiritually. They wanted to help children understand our rapidly changing world, an aim that sounded modern and open-minded, and to help them use language effectively and imaginatively, when they read, wrote and spoke. In addition, they were keen that girls as well as boys should have a good basic knowledge of maths, science and history, and to make them aware of 'God's created world'. Few parents would want less for their child, but having spent time in the school myself I know that not all these worthy aims in the school's handbook translated into reality in the classroom.

It didn't take me long to discover that the school's regime remained as strict and as regimented as it had been when I was there, and children were still not allowed to talk in the classroom or while eating their lunch. Although corporal punishment was banned in state schools in 1986, it only became illegal in private schools in 2002 and until that time teachers at Tadford smacked pupils when they felt it was necessary to do so.

Black repeatedly denied this. In an interview with a journalist in our local paper he stated that, although like many people he had at times wanted to smack a child – mentioning that he came from a generation for whom it was completely normal to have been smacked when young – he had never, ever done so. He must have conveniently 'forgot' that corporal punishment was practised not only by all of the school teachers, but also by himself.

Black was also recorded delivering a sermon in which he said, 'How do you correct a child who you feel is doing something wrong, something that is against God's will? I'll tell you how. You beat it out of them. It happened to me when I was young, and look at me now. Do you not think that this is part of God's plan?' He then went on to repeat one of his favourite sayings: 'Use the rod and save the child.'

It was impossible to move your children to another school once you were a member of the Church. In another sermon Black castigated state schools and the teachers who worked in them, saying, 'It's no wonder that children turn out so badly when a bunch of filthy left-wing homosexuals are teaching them at school. Parents should know this. Their children's teachers are like swine possessed by devils.' Nor were the children even allowed to go to Cubs or Brownies.

Paul was quiet and struggled in school, largely because of his dysgraphia, but Rebecca had a very different temperament. Boisterous, loud and highly intelligent, she was also extremely short-sighted, accident-prone, difficult to discipline and very impatient. She found it difficult to wait for her turn at anything, whether it was to go down a slide or be served with her school lunch. Her personality meant she had a very different relationship with her father. Although Peter loved both children he was particularly close to Paul because he was so easy-going. He was more judgemental of Rebecca and had a shorter fuse with her.

Rebecca's attitude also got her into a lot of trouble at school.

Punishments for school-age children were adminis-tered according to the number of 'forfeits' or failings a pupil was given. More than two demerits in a day resulted in a detention. Two detentions in a week led to a 'whacking', a word that was part of Tadford terminology and meant a spanking or beating with a trainer or gym shoe.

Parents would be notified when a punishment was about to be administered. The child in question would be given an orange forfeit slip to take home and show their parents if they had misbehaved once during the school day and a red slip if they had misbehaved twice.

I tried to hide from Peter the forfeit slips the children were given so that he wouldn't smack them. It worked for a while and then the teachers decided to record forfeits in each child's school diary, along with what they needed to bring the next day. We had to sign these notes, so Peter saw them and would often spank the children first.

Offences punished by forfeit included: not wearing the exact school uniform, not having the correct hairstyle, or being muddy; not having trimmed fingernails; not eating all the school dinner; answering back; being late; and not reciting or writing out 'memory verses' from the Bible perfectly. Pupils would also be punished if they were late for church, even when it was obviously their parents' fault, were noisy or took inadequate notes of the services. I remember Luke getting a demerit for flicking a bee, Daniel for coughing too loudly during an assembly even though he had a bad cold, Rebecca for going down a slide the wrong way, and Paul for having his hair parted incorrectly according to the school rules.

Other punishable offences included not producing work to a sufficiently high standard in school. Pupils over 6 years old had homework every evening and would be in trouble if this was judged unsatisfactory.

Corporal punishment was not supposed to start until children reached primary-school age, but I saw for myself how children of under school age were taken to the toilet and smacked by their teacher. Both Paul and Rebecca remember being smacked in pre-school too, but neither of them told me at the time. They later explained that they didn't dare in case they got another smack from their father, or even me. Children under four had a rest period each afternoon and were expected to sleep. If they weren't tired they had to pretend to be. Teachers were strict about nap time, and if the children moved or messed around they got smacked on their bottom.

One of the most common reasons for being smacked was not eating all the school dinner within the half-hour allowed. Some children were constantly in trouble because they ate slowly. Others suffered only when they were ill and had no appetite. Rebecca, who was permanently hungry and eventually grew to be 5 ft 11 in. tall, was rarely in trouble for this offence. She could eat for Britain and nearly always went up for seconds. Paul managed to escape punishment too, even though he ate like a snail and didn't have a big appetite. Luckily he usually managed to finish just within the time limit.

Both children were most frequently punished for not accurately reciting and writing down their biblical verses. Every week children of 6 and older were given twelve verses from the New International Version Bible to memorize. I had to do the same when I was at school but luckily I was much older than they were before it was thrust on me.

Nearly all the children struggled, but the task was particularly hard for Paul because he was dysgraphic. For a short period he had special one-to-one lessons from a kind teacher who understood that it was almost impossible for him to write down a passage from memory totally accurately, word for word and comma for comma and with everything correctly spelt. When he made a mistake while practising the teacher would touch his hand and show him what he had done wrong and it made him want to do better. He thought it was grossly unfair of the teachers to give him a forfeit when they knew he had a recognized condition that wasn't his fault.

Rebecca described the task as 'a nightmare'. She believed a child had better things to do after school than read a passage from the Bible over and over again until he or she could remember it. She said she couldn't do it to save her life and as a result got countless forfeits and whacks. As Rebecca got older she became fiercely critical of the ethos of the Church. She felt it was so restricted and regimented it didn't let a child be a child and do normal childish things. She hated the fact that girls couldn't, for example, watch TV or dress up or play with dolls, and there was only a small selection of books that had a religious theme that she could read. She was angry she wasn't allowed to have friends outside Church and that everything she did – school, meals, activities and social life – all had to happen within the Church. But she particularly hated having to keep her blazer on all the time, apart from sports periods, even in summer when it was baking hot, so that she always looked smart.

Paul, like all the others, hated his beatings. The teacher would drag him into a room at the back of the school and tell him to drop his trousers and pants and bend over. Sometimes there would be another teacher present, at other times not. After the beatings he wouldn't want to sit down for the next twenty minutes or so, but it was the humiliation and embarrassment that really hurt him.

All his school mates knew what had happened. He remembered one occasion when a teacher took him for a beating into an empty classroom that had a large window. Within a few seconds his entire class came to watch what was happening and he could see their eyes fixated on his bottom. He believed the teacher must have seen them all too, but still it didn't stop him. It was also an unwritten rule that children didn't cry.

When Paul was 8 he developed a problem with lower stomach pain. It worried me sick and I took him to the doctor, but he couldn't find anything physically wrong. In retrospect Paul believes it was caused by stress. He said the continual smacking was too much for him to handle and he was permanently scared about being smacked again, which couldn't have been healthy. His view makes sense as he never had the pain during the school holidays.

Rebecca understood that smacking was part of the way Tadford operated, but it offended her keen sense of justice that she could get into trouble for things that were beyond her control. She used to suffer from head-aches, which I also think were stress-related. One day she was in such pain that she couldn't work. She explained to the teacher what was wrong, but instead of taking her to the school nurse he gave her a forfeit, which led to a spanking.

When she was 8 she was hit for using a swear word that she heard someone say in the street one day and repeated in school without having any idea what it meant. No one explained what she had done wrong, so she had no idea for some while why she had got into trouble.

She was also whacked on the hand with a ruler after a maths test, even though she'd got all the answers right. The teacher said she had cheated by copying another child's work, but Rebecca insisted that this child was sitting in another part of the room and she couldn't have seen what he was doing even if she'd wanted to. Rebecca also had a bed-wetting problem, which she thinks was an additional result of stress. I was so worried about her that I took her to the doctor, but tests showed that there was nothing medically wrong.

Rebecca could wet the bed as often as three or four times a night. When I heard her cry, I'd rush to her room and change the bedcovers and her nightie before Peter heard her, and try to reassure her by saying it didn't matter. But if Peter found out, he would give her a smack on the bottom with a bedroom slipper or a shoe, which was so unfair as she was half asleep and didn't really know what was going on. It was also counterproductive as it made Rebecca more nervous and worsened the problem. She later said to me, 'Why didn't Daddy think there might be a reason why I was wetting the bed and sit down and talk to me?' Luke also wet the bed and Peter repeatedly smacked him too. Luckily for him, Daniel never suffered from this problem.

I tried to talk to Peter about it, but I was frightened that he would lose his temper with me.

Despite it all, however, I knew Peter was basically a decent man, and I thought that he was doing the right thing and that it was what the Church expected. He had, after all, a ringing endorsement from Black and senior Church members who believed not only that parents who disciplined their children proved their love for them, but also that they were bringing them up in the way of God. It was made very clear to us that we had to be strict at home to match the standards of the Church. It meant that any efforts I made to stop Peter had absolutely no effect. I couldn't even confide my overwhelming anxieties to anyone or ask for advice as it would have been reported back to the Church leaders and I would have been hauled before them and demolished.

To my great shame I smacked my children too, although never very hard. It highlights how much power Black exerted over me that I felt so compelled to obey him that I did something that went totally against my maternal instinct. My only justification was that I didn't dare not hit them for fear they would go to Hell. It was only much later that I realized how barbaric and unnecessary it was. I often ask myself how I could have allowed them to suffer in this way and I still can't really explain it. I do know that I often think about it and shudder in horror. I know, too, that I will never forgive myself for what they went through, but I realize that anyone who

157

has not been exposed to the various and constant pressures practised by Tadford at the time would find it even more difficult to understand.

Chapter 8

The Church Demands

B y this time I was collapsing under the pressure of my life. Not only was I the main carer for our four small children, but I was also working at least five days a week for the Church, often doing weeding or heavy lifting in the allotment, and helping Peter with the language teaching business that he had set up on the side. Not surprisingly the strain took its toll. I struggled to produce enough milk for both Luke and Daniel. When they were six months old I had to stop breastfeeding entirely because I simply couldn't cope with feeding both of them. This upset me greatly as I felt that I wasn't providing for them as a good mother should.

It was during this same month that I came home from shopping and found Peter in our bedroom smacking Luke on his bare bottom, whilst Daniel was cowering in the corner. A wave of rage and panic swept through me as I looked first at Peter, then at Luke's tiny bottom, and saw to my horror that it already looked bruised. It was a hideous, devastating sight and in a supreme act of self-control I stopped myself from screaming at Peter and instead calmly walked up to him, bent down, and took both Luke and Daniel in my arms. I then sat on the floor in a corner of the room with my back pressed up against the wall. Tears ran down my cheeks as I held them close to me for ages, all the while thinking, 'My little baby has a heart murmur. This can't be right.'

I didn't dare discuss my anxiety with anyone in the Church. Nor was it appropriate to discuss something so intimate with our neighbour Dinah, particularly as she wasn't a Christian and wouldn't have understood the demands of the Church. Nor, to her credit, did she ever ask.

And I didn't consider talking to my parents, as I hardly saw them. At the most they would come twice a year and stay a day or two. Their visits were always a time of tension between Peter and me. I could sense he still felt uncomfortable with them because they were not members of Tadford and could influence me in the wrong way. It all meant they were never welcome. This reached a head a few months after the twins were born. My mother had visited immediately after the birth, but Dad hadn't been able to join her, so we made an arrangement for them to come down to see them together. They were looking forward to the trip enormously, but shortly before they were due to arrive Peter told me that Black said they weren't to stay with us because they might try to manipulate me. I felt too embarrassed to tell them myself, but Peter rang and told them why they couldn't stay. Dinah kindly offered to put them up and looked after them marvellously, as she also did on subsequent occasions. Only recently has Dad confessed that, although they were comfortable while staying with Dinah, not being welcome in his daughter's home made him believe he was not good enough for me. I felt dreadful.

I remember that during one weekend visit we all went to church together on the Sunday and Black made an extraordinary comment about a young woman who recently married and went to live up north, saying he couldn't understand why she wanted to live in such a forsaken hole, adding that perhaps she wanted to go to Hell. It's hard to imagine it was just coincidence that he spoke so rudely about the part of the country where my parents lived.

Peter was just as withdrawn and non-communicative with my sister as he had been with my parents. Kerry had moved to Canada with her husband after gaining her doctorate and was working as an occupational therapist. She came back every so often to visit the family and see me, and always said I looked exhausted and that she was worried about me. Like my parents, she didn't feel welcome, but like them she always came to Sunday assemblies. She was appalled when during one service she heard Black say that the death of someone was the result of their going against God's will.

She also felt very concerned about my narrow-mindedness. She told me later that she thought I was totally brainwashed, but refused to give up on me. Whenever she suggested visiting, both Peter and I would say it wasn't convenient, but she wouldn't take no for an answer and came anyway. She kept insisting it was wrong that I was being told what to do in every area of my life, and that I was being ruled by fear and control rather than kindness.

I was totally unreceptive to Kerry's comments and to my later shame I once called her a sinner and told her she didn't want to know the truth. To her credit, she realized that the words I used were almost identical to those she had heard Black utter when she attended assemblies at Tadford, and took no notice. She didn't argue with me, but calmly stood her ground and only much later told me she found it heartbreaking to see how much I was missing out in life. Luckily, she never gave up on me.

In retrospect perhaps my sister's efforts did have an effect on my subconscious because when the twins were

2 I began very slowly to see my life slightly more objectively. It was almost as if imperceptibly, somewhere at the back of my brain, thoughts of my own, rather than those forced upon me, slowly began to grow. It was rather like an old machine that had been neglected for years gradually coming back to life, and it took several more years before these thoughts formed into something tangible and more positive.

This coincided with my move from the allotment to work in the Church bookshop, which, like Black's publishing business, was run by Holy Bloom. I established a routine of dropping the children off at school or the crèche to arrive at the shop by 8.30 a.m. I'd work until 3.15 p.m. and then pick them up from school.

The bookshop was in one of two rooms located on the side of the warehouse nearest the main road. In the room immediately off the corridor we sold religious books produced by Black's company, Bibles, CDs of his sermons, and gifts and ornaments. In the second room, accessible through the bookshop, we ran a busy café. It was decorated with chintzy wallpaper and was a popular place for people to have a snack or a piece of home-made cake. I was expected to bake cakes for the shop and to pay for all the ingredients, but all the money from selling them went straight to Tadford. Two other mothers worked with me and we'd take it in turns to be in the kitchen, or the computer room dealing with stock, do the cleaning, or serve food and drink. I was also on the Church work rota and was expected to clean the school classrooms and toilets once a month, and feed a visiting family of up to six at my own expense once a month on a Sunday.

Meanwhile, Peter's career was going well. Although his TEFL work had dropped off recently, he had been promoted at the fitness club and was now responsible for training pupils that came from a number of local schools and clubs that didn't have the financial wherewithal to buy expensive multigyms. This was good news but it meant that he came home exhausted as the sessions often ran during out-of-school hours. He'd eat a meal I'd prepared, and then go out to do Church work, sometimes not returning until 1 a.m. He hardly ever even sat with us in assemblies as he also worked in a room next to the church hall recording and then editing Black's sermons. He was absent so often that one of the regular visitors asked me if I was a single parent. There was never any time for us to put our family's emotional or financial needs before the demands of the Church.

To add insult to injury, despite our long working hours we still found it difficult to make ends meet. I blamed the huge amount we had to hand over to the Church. Apart from paying tithes, we paid a considerable amount per month in school fees. School lunch was extra and we even had to pay a lost property fine of 50p to retrieve an article bearing a name tag and £1 for an unnamed article. It doesn't sound much but it all added up, particularly as the children lost their things all the time.

So, despite Peter's promotion, we were still finding it hard to make ends meet. I am not by nature a jealous person but it did niggle that while we were struggling, Black enjoyed a luxurious lifestyle, with an income that came from several sources, including the Church and various directorships. He was also living rent-free in a house owned by the Church. He had an entertainment budget, travelled first-class wherever he went and drove a smart BMW with leather seats that was worth considerably more than Peter earned in a year. Heather and his two sons and two daughters also had their own top-of-the-range cars.

The July weekend conference was always popular and the one held that year was no exception. Several hundred visitors turned up and Black again told them and Church members alike that Tadford was the only place where God was. I don't know how many of them considered logically why, if this was so, there was no reference in the Bible to Tadford being the only true Church. Equally, if it was, why did God wait so many years before he found somewhere in which he felt sufficiently comfortable to perform his miracles? It certainly didn't occur to me. Instead I listened as Black followed his pronouncement with the words: 'If you do not see miracles happening in your church it means that the church is not with Jesus and Jesus is not with the church. To those of you who wish to see miracles I say this. Go and seek another church.' He rubbed in the point, adding, 'There are many false teachers out there, just as there are false prophets. But when you see miracles performed you will know that you have come home to Jesus.'

He was particularly critical of people on state benefits. He made little distinction between the unfortunate and the idle, describing both as 'robbers', and decreed that they should be treated according to the biblical text that says 'those who do not work, shall not eat'. He also commended regimes in the Third World for knowing what to do with homosexuals, namely 'taking from them the life for which they are unworthy'.

Black was now spending a considerable amount of time travelling round the globe taking his message to the people. His two most popular destinations were South India and an evangelical university in the United States founded by a renowned evangelist after whom it was named. His souvenirs from these trips were often honorary degrees. He was, for example, made an Honorary Doctor of Divinity by a university in India – which is only recognized locally – and an Honorary Doctor of Divinity by the American university, which is only recognized regionally. Other similar honorary degrees soon followed. I felt increasingly cynical about this ever-growing string of honorary qualifications, some of which seem to have been acquired almost overnight without the traditional hard work, rigorous study and examinations that most church leaders put themselves through. Despite his obvious pride in his qualifications, he was careful not to use them in some of his business documents.

Black was on intimate terms with several American televangelists, and copied many of their practices. When Black had set up Tadford College the previous year, a university-level institute that offered BA degrees in theology, he flew over to the States to speak with officials at evangelical universities and secure affiliation with them. Black also had a wide range of contacts in South India, where there is a large Charismatic movement. It was a common sight to see Indian preachers stand up on the stage at Tadford and preach, and on the whole they were more convincing, and I should add, more spiritual than Black.

Peter was involved in sorting out the plumbing for Black's new home, which kept him busier than ever. Once the house was refurbished everyone who was invited round could see that it was an amazing place. It had five bedrooms, all with fitted cupboards and en-suite bathrooms, a large office, an enormous lounge with a giant television, which was very unusual then, a spacious, fully equipped kitchen and a good-sized garden. The interior decoration was very plush and many of the religious-themed paintings that hung on the walls had been made by a member of Tadford.

Black used his new home for the Church as well as himself. I and others went to dinner there soon after he moved in and we were offered a generous buffet of wonderful salads, cold meats and pasta. Peter and I had also moved – we bought a two-bedroom house in a quiet cul de sac in a new development – so that Peter could be closer to his fitness centre, although we were still not far from the church.

Thinking of the future, we decided to convert the house to a six-bedroom house so that each of our children would have a room of their own, with one spare room for anyone who came to visit. Almost inevitably the building work took longer and cost more than we had anticipated. The conversion took many months and we finally decided we would definitely move in before Christmas, even though it still looked like a building site. By now I had become so used to life in the shadow of the Church that it was where I felt most comfortable and, although I was often unhappy about some of its more controlling aspects, day to day I tried to get on with my life in a positive way. I had gradually gathered around me a warm, loving circle of mothers who had similar-aged children. But there was an unspoken understanding that our friendships would only last as long as we all toed the line. If any of us criticized the regime or Black himself she risked being ostracized. I tried to keep any misgivings to myself and never confided in anyone because I knew that their loyalty would always be to the Church rather than to an individual.

On the surface, at least, we had the same aims and beliefs, and everyone knew we had to get on because we didn't have any other friends. It meant I saw the same people all the time, which was a bit claustrophobic, but, on the other hand, the children always had friends to play with and we would meet regularly as a group for a picnic or coffee.

When we weren't arguing about the time he spent working at the Church, Peter and I got on well too. As a couple we were closest to Peter's cousin Carol and her husband, Simon Russell, who married shortly after we did. Socially we were very restricted in what we could do: we weren't allowed to go to the cinema, theatre or nightclubs, but we enjoyed long walks in the country and sometimes went out for a pizza or a curry.

My concept of what made up a happy marriage was based on my parents, who were wonderful together despite their trials with my brother and my mother's attempt to move to Tadford. My father was always there for my mother, quiet and loving, and almost never raised his voice. They were openly affectionate with each other and didn't seem bothered that they didn't have much money.

My marriage, by contrast, was fundamentally lonely, because Peter was never there. I felt overwhelmed by the four children and almost as if I were a single parent. Even the white wedding I had looked forward to since I was a child had been ruined by the arguments over the date and the choice of bridesmaids. Not long after the birth of the twins Peter's workload for the Church was causing almost continual rows between us and we were called into Black's office. Hugh Porter was there and both men told me I would be moving from working at the bookshop to joining Peter in the recording room, where he spent evenings and weekends editing Black's sermons. They said it was a good way for us to spend more time together. I am not sure how much sense this made as I would mainly be working during the day, but there was no discussion. It was presented to me as a done deal.

Black was a relentless promoter of both himself and the Church, which were basically the same thing, and the church hall had microphones dangling from the ceiling and a photographer was always on hand. The recording suite, situated in a small room within the church, was lavishly fitted out with equipment for recording and editing Black's sermons. There were cables everywhere and, as with the church hall itself, the room got so hot that the Church installed air-conditioning to stop the recording equipment – and the workers themselves – overheating.

Despite the fact that I had no relevant experience or training, I was immediately expected to produce a constant stream of recordings of every single sermon that Black made, as well as record question and answer sessions that took place in the church when other preachers – often from the States or South India – came to visit us. If I was not working hard or quickly enough Black would tell me off. Some of the recordings needed a great deal of skill and time to produce. It was not just the editing: I was expected to interview people, plan the scripts and design CD covers. It was a very time-consuming job and, perhaps as Black and Hugh Porter anticipated, I began regularly working with Peter on those evenings when he was not too exhausted from taking fitness classes, as well as at weekends. We would even sometimes put the children down to sleep in a room next door if there was no babysitter available, in order to be able to work through the night.

I thought I did pretty well. I tried to earn Black's praise and be accepted as a good, hard-working member of the Church, but he never really thanked me or seemed grateful. Just before Christmas he again called Peter and me into his office and reprimanded us for not producing enough recordings. He also complained that CD sales were low. I was furious because I was working as hard as I could, and I stuck up for myself. This was regarded as a rebellious act. You were not expected to argue with Black, and I could see that Peter was embarrassed by my behaviour. But I didn't care and at one point I was so angry I marched out of the room.

I felt Black's criticism was basically unfair. It was taking me hours to remove the worst of his strong language and character defamations to make sure the recordings were fit for public consumption. For example, he described a Hindu who refused to renounce his faith as 'a spineless idiot' and declared that visiting a nightclub was like 'entering the bowels of Hell'. I also recorded and edited his 'miracles', when he would pronounce a person cured, with no written evidence or reference to a doctor.

One of his 'healing miracles' was for a young girl called Jess Atkins, who suffered from a rare bone cancer called osteosarcoma. I believe Jess's parents were told about the Church and its miracles by a Church member who was a primary-school teacher and who taught Jess. They brought her along a few times and were clearly utterly devoted to their little girl and very distressed by how ill she was. She then became extremely poorly and at one point was given just days to live. Black went to visit her in hospital and subsequently claimed that she had been miraculously healed. Soon afterwards Tadford sold recordings promoting the fact. Sadly Jess died five years later but the Church continued to sell the CD.

Some months after Jess's tragic death an ex-member of Tadford made a formal complaint to the Church about the ongoing sale of the CD. A disclaimer was then added to it stating that the girl had died of complications following a bacterial infection, an illness unrelated to her disease. Even though this infection was not mentioned on her death certificate Black was not to be thwarted and then argued that the child had died of another form of cancer unrelated to the one that had been 'healed'.

Black also claimed he had successfully prayed for a man with polio to be cured, and although he was still seeing his consultant and was very poorly, I had to write an introduction to one of Black's presentations and present the man in such a manner as to suggest that he had been healed. I felt very guilty doing so, almost as if I was colluding in a terrible untruth. I had to convince myself that even if he had only improved psychologically through Black's prayers, he was on the way to being healed, but I didn't feel remotely comfortable about it. I hated feeling I was complicit in helping to deceive people. I didn't want to encourage them to come to church to see the wonderful miracles Jesus could do for them, when I knew what was happening wasn't a miracle at all. I struggled with it, but didn't know what to do.

To make sure he had a steady flow of unwell individuals to 'cure', Black advertised in specific publications that acted as support structures for people with debilitating illnesses, offering a miracle cure if they visited Tadford. This bothered me too as it felt like preying on the vulnerable.

It took me years to find an explanation that made sense of it all. This was that when miraculous healing allegedly takes place in religious settings like Tadford there is usually a lot of hype, including clapping, singing, dancing and shouting. These all produce adrenaline, a natural form of morphine, and endorphins, which are natural pain and stress fighters. When someone is prayed over, and, for example, told to lift an arm that they haven't been able to lift for months, they can do so because their body has produced this natural form of morphine. The trouble is that the next day, when the natural morphine has worn off, the condition and the pain return. Sometimes they are even worse than they were before the healing, as the person has done things with their arm they shouldn't have done.

The other explanation is that they get a 'high' from what they believe is a great spiritual experience. This is followed by a low, so understandably they want to come to another meeting to get another high, and the whole process can be addictive. Equally, if the individual doesn't feel better after all the attention, he or she can feel it is their fault. If the mood of the group is that healing is happening, no one wants to rock the boat, especially in a church like Tadford where people dress the same, say the same, do the same and think the same.

One of the busiest times of the year for the promotional CDs Peter and I worked on was the spring conference. Church regulars added to the large numbers of visitors and there were several bishops dressed in flowing robes. The large church hall was transformed into a banqueting room before each meal to accommodate all the guests for their lunch and dinner, and then all the tables and chairs were quickly swept away and replaced by the usual church furniture before the assemblies were held. Peter and I, however, stayed in the recording room throughout the conference, solidly editing because Black wanted the CDs ready by the end of the three-day gathering. I got someone to look after the children, but no one even thought to bring us food. I had to dash home and grab something, otherwise we would have starved. As it was, we did one 48-hour session without any sleep. It was a horrendous task, not least because Black's sermons were so repetitive and he ranted against so many things that we'd sometimes have only about ten minutes of usable material after hours and hours of recording.

Some time before the end of the event, when I was utterly exhausted, I decided this wasn't a life I wanted. A few days afterwards I was in the recording room printing off the covers for the CD boxes and still feeling shattered, when Peter and I and several other parents were called to a parents' meeting. There we were reminded that we weren't allowed to go on holiday without first asking permission from either Black or Hugh Porter. It was emphasized that we were banned from going away when conferences were being held, which took place several times a year. As well as the regular annual spring, July weekend and Christmas conferences, most years there were also a men's conference, a woman's conference, a bishops' conference and sometimes others as well. We couldn't go away for a weekend during term time as Sunday-morning attendance at Church was compulsory. It was occasionally possible to have a week or so away during the school summer holidays, but we were often either too busy with our workload for the Church or didn't have enough money.

Not long after this parents' meeting, Kerry, who had flown over from Canada, exploded in anger and said that Tadford was 'getting to be like a bloody cult'. I'd known deep inside for a long time that something wasn't right with the Church, but it had never once occurred to me that I was somewhere that could be described as a cult. From then on the wheels in my brain started to turn and all sorts of things began to click into place, including why Tadford had never been part of the local community. Most churches work within their local area helping the aged and visiting the sick and needy, but I don't remember Tadford ever doing that. It was all about recruiting new members, praising Black and raising money, while he showed utter contempt for other church leaders and regularly referred to them as, at best, 'buffoons'.

Around this time other churches in the area were also becoming concerned about Black's pronouncements and the way Tadford Charismatic Church was behaving towards its members.

I could now hear two conflicting voices in my head. One wanted to be accepted and loved by the Church community, which had become my home and all I knew. I had no concept of any other way of life. It was also the place Peter fervently loved. The other voice constantly queried what was going on, but it was only after I visited the Christian bookshop in town that a light finally went on in my brain. I knew I had to get out, but if you were as brainwashed, intimidated and suppressed as I was, it took a long time to dare to find the courage to take action. Perhaps because my parents insisted I stay at Tadford and I hadn't come of my own free will in the belief that it was an extraordinary place,

I'd never let Black totally control my brain. But I'd always been afraid of him and believed that would never change.

Chapter 9

My Eyes Are Opened

*I*n normal circumstances if someone no longer wants to be a member of an organization, they leave, especially if their children's welfare is at stake. But it wasn't nearly so simple or straightforward for me. I was afraid God would be angry with me if I went away. I also had so much invested in Tadford that it wasn't easy to give it up. My husband, whom I loved despite everything, was happy there, my four children were used to the Church school, despite its standards of discipline, and I loved my home.

Besides, I didn't have a clue where to go. I'd kept my parents and sister at a distance for so long I no longer felt close to them, and I'd lost touch with all my early teenage friends. Despite my fears, something deep inside me propelled me forward and gave me strength. It helped that Kath, who had come to the bookshop with me, had been so shocked by what she read about cults that she, her husband Robin and their three small children left Tadford almost immediately and none of them had so far dropped dead. But I argued irrationally with myself that it might be different for them as, unlike me, they had been members of the Church for only a year and didn't feel so intimidated. Kath and I continued to meet for coffee and she tried to support me.

By this time I was also increasingly worried about the children, who now sometimes hid behind the sofa when their father came in from work in case he wanted to smack them. Luke was particularly affected and if he was having a meal when Peter came through the front door he'd look panicky, start to pant and eat very fast. I would try to get him to eat before Peter came home, but it was not always possible. Sometimes Peter would be so strict about the children finishing everything that he would even tell them off for not drinking all their squash. I dreaded meal times and found each one traumatic. One day Peter found a pile of mouldy, half-eaten sandwiches behind the fridge in the kitchen. Luke hadn't been able to finish them and had hidden them so he wouldn't get a smack. I was really shocked as I'd had no idea what he was doing, but that didn't stop Peter giving him another firm spanking.

I had hidden *When a Church Becomes a Cult* in my underwear drawer because I knew Peter would never look for anything there, and after Kath and her husband left the Church, I carefully took it out from its hiding place.

The children were at school, Peter was at work and it felt relatively safe for me to go through it again. Towards the end of the book it mentioned an organization that ran a helpline for people who had become involved with religious cults and who were seeking advice and support. I took a deep breath, double-locked the front door, picked up the phone, dialled 141 to prevent my number registering and made the most significant phone call of my life. I was answered by Adam, the helpline's general secretary.

'I am sorry to bother you,' I began, my heart pounding with fear, 'but I am desperate. I know I shouldn't speak to you but I must. My name is Sarah. I am too afraid to tell you where I am calling from but I need help. I think I am in a cult. My family and I live within a mile of the church and my children go to the Church school.' Then I faltered, adding quietly, 'I don't know what to do'.

'I know what you are talking about,' Adam replied.

My voice rose with anxiety as I said, 'You can't. I haven't told you where I live.'

'You are a member of Tadford Charismatic Church, aren't you?' he asked.

I was so shocked I burst into tears. Adam gently told me he had known about Tadford for many years and could recommend someone who could help me. He gave me the phone number of a charitable organization that provided counselling and support to people and their families who felt damaged by extremist religious groups and cults. He told me to speak to its director, a man called Clive, and said I could also call him at any time. I then rang my parents, my hands trembling so much I could hardly dial the number.

'Dad,' I said, without pausing to even ask how he was, 'I think I'm in a cult.' He was completely taken aback but spoke cautiously to me, telling me that he and Mum had been unhappy for a long time about how Tadford had been treating people, but felt they couldn't say anything to me until I had a more open mind.

He then passed me over to Mum and we both burst into tears. Suddenly, after all the years of near estrangement, I felt an instant and powerful connection with her again. She felt it too, and told me she loved me and that her heart went out to me. I felt so reassured that my parents were pleased at the chance of having their daughter back and that they would help me, despite the fact we had been distant for so long.

I knew I had to call Clive next, but I had made two private calls from home and I didn't dare make a third. Peter always looked carefully through our phone bills and queried numbers he didn't instantly recognize. I jumped into the car and drove a few miles away so that I was less likely to be recognized, and only stopped when

I reached a suitably out-of-the-way phone box. I rang Clive but I was so nervous I couldn't feed the coins in properly and we kept getting cut off. Luckily he called me back. We talked for about an hour and he calmed me down. He said that I should try to come to London, where he worked, to see him. When we'd finished talking I felt a huge weight lift from my shoulders. I realized that my thoughts and feelings were genuine and that I wasn't a heretic or an evil person.

Inevitably this confirmation made me feel sick in my stomach. I felt as if I were standing on the edge of a huge chasm that into which I could tumble at any moment and it was far too complex for me to work out instantly what to do with all this new information.

I then tried to bring myself back to the present and rushed into work, but I was so emotionally drained I couldn't concentrate properly on anything. It was as if all the years of being at Tadford had melted away and all the feelings I had had about the Church not being a good place when my parents first left me there had resurfaced. This time, however, I knew that if anyone discovered my feelings both I and the children would be at risk. Not least because I also knew Tadford always tried to help whichever member of a separating couple stayed within the Church to fight for custody.

By the time I went to collect the children from school, I had managed to compose myself, on the outside at least. I didn't even mention anything to Peter when he came home from work. I thought it best to learn as much as I could about cults, so that I would be able to discuss them with him in a way that would make him want to come out of Tadford with me. My priority was for us to remain a family. I so wanted to believe that all our troubles were the result of his working too hard. As a committed Christian I believed marriage was for life. Peter was my husband and the father of my children and the vows we took on our wedding day, especially 'Until death us do part', were engraved on my heart.

I was unusually quiet but Peter was as busy as usual and went out after his dinner without noticing anything was wrong. It shows how badly we were communicating. I barely slept that night, and tossed and turned for hours, but he didn't notice that either. Or if he did he didn't say anything. My wakefulness was useful, though, as I came up with a reason to go to London. I occasionally had my hair cut in a salon there and told Peter I thought it was time for me to go again. He barely reacted. A week later, with my hair freshly re-styled, I was sitting in Clive's London office trembling with anticipation and fear. He had asked me to bring both our business and my personal bank statements with me, and they were in a large white envelope on my lap.

At first I felt very tense, as I was confronting many different aspects of my life for the first time since I had been at Tadford. But Clive made me feel at ease, especially once he told me he was a long-time member of his local choir and a committed Anglican. It felt more natural to talk to someone who had a religious background. I told him that Black claimed that Tadford was the only place where God was and he replied, 'That's what all cults say.' He also said that he didn't like using the word 'cult', preferring the term 'abusive group', and that he believed Tadford was a group that abused and damaged people.

I confided in Clive that I thought Peter treated me harshly because he thought I was rebellious and wanted to get me under control. We then talked about money and how difficult it had become to make ends meet. Together we looked through some of the bank statements and he commented on the large amounts that were going out as tithes and school fees. He wasn't surprised that we found life financially tough.

He also recommended I read two books: *Captive Hearts, Captive Minds: Freedom and Recovery from Cults and Abusive Relationships* by Madeleine Landau Tobias and Janja Lalich, and *Cults in Our Midst: The Continuing Fight Against Their Hidden Menace* by Margaret Thaler Singer. He gave me a copy of the second.

We talked for at least an hour and Clive said he was there to support me and that I could ring him at any time, then recommended I buy a phone card so I could call him from anywhere in the country without the number registering. He also suggested that if I had time I should go and see a specialist lawyer called Wendy, whose office was close by. I didn't really have the time, but as she was free I didn't want to miss the opportunity.

Wendy was sympathetic, concise and to the point. She said she needed evidence that would safeguard me and the children if anything ever went to court. She told me to let her have the children's birth certificates and their passports so that they couldn't be taken out of the country by anyone but me. She also asked for unedited tapes of Black's sermons and 'miracle healings', and pointed out that although I wanted Peter to leave Tadford so we could still be a family, I had to both plan for the possibility that he wouldn't come with me as well as gather evidence to prevent him getting custody of the children.

I knew Tadford would aim for custody not because they cared about the children, but because it would be a victory over me. Wendy also asked me for various documents relating to the school, including the children's signed diary books, their forfeit slips and the notes they took during church services. She also advised me to try to live normally, so I wouldn't arouse suspicion. By the time we'd finished talking I was quite agitated that I might be late for the children and my secret trip would be discovered, but luckily I was on time and all was well.

I put *Cults in Our Midst* in the same underwear drawer where I'd hidden the book about cults by Stephen Wookey.

I immediately started accumulating evidence for Wendy and the next day went to the recording room as soon as I had taken the children to school. I locked the door and picked out an unedited recording and began copying it onto a blank CD. When I had finished, I put it into my handbag, sneaked downstairs and hid the disk in the boot underneath the spare wheel of our old, battered Ford. I tried to copy one CD a day but made sure I paid £1 into the tithe box in the church for each of the blank CDs I used. I didn't want to be accused of stealing. Later, when I had the chance, I posted them to my parents for safekeeping.

I also copied unedited recordings of Black preaching about people dropping dead when they turned against him or the Church, and of him touting for large sums of money. This too went smoothly and I surprised myself that I could put on such a calm-I'm-doing-nothing-and-everything-is-fine front. What really made me nervous was deciding when to talk to Peter. The timing was vital and it took me a month to pluck up the courage.

Finally I chose a Thursday night in May because Peter had come back from church at 10 p.m., which was quite early for him. I was very nervous and began by saying we needed to talk and suggested we sit in the lounge. I waited until he seemed settled and then told him that I believed we were in a cult. I then handed him *Cults in Our Midst* and *When a Church Becomes a Cult*, and suggested he read them. He looked at me strangely but took the books and flicked through the pages, stopping to read various passages.

Neither of us spoke for a couple of hours but then just before midnight he put the books down, looked me in the eyes, and said I was right that we were in a cult and we should leave together. I could hardly believe it, and a huge wave of excitement and relief coursed through me. My Peter would come with me and we would stay together as a proper family. I slept well for the first time in weeks and woke up early to start planning our future. Often I would go to bed before Peter came home from working at the church, but for the next few days I stayed up and we talked intimately about our future. I suggested we could move to a town in another county that had a fitness club affiliated to the one at which Peter was working and where he knew the boss. He felt pretty sure that he would be offered work there, as he had a reputation for being an excellent coach. We both wanted to live in the country, agreed it was a beautiful area and Peter said it was a good idea. We also agreed that the children were too young to understand the implications of leaving Tadford and that we wouldn't tell them until all our plans were made. I was pleased as I didn't think they could keep it secret and I didn't want Black to know.

I felt so happy and close to Peter and this reinforced my view that our terrible rows had far more to do with faults in the Church than in our own relationship. I felt so proud that he had the courage to agree to something that was so contrary to the beliefs he had until now stood by, and that he had done so purely on the evidence of the books I had shown him. I also suggested I should look into possible schools and houses in the area we'd agreed on, and again Peter consented. The following day I rang several estate agents and Church of England schools. I felt it was important for the children to maintain a religious background so that a change would be less traumatic for them. Over the next few weeks we continued to plan, but I noticed Peter showed less and less enthusiasm and, although he didn't say anything, I could feel him slowly withdrawing from me. He also kept stopping me from criticizing the Church.

I wouldn't let myself ask him if he had discussed our conversations and plans with his aunt but, as she ruled the roost in their family, I presumed he had done so. And if she knew, then Black, who had just returned from a preaching trip abroad, would certainly have been told the minute he returned. I rang Clive for advice. His main aim, he said, was to help Peter and me be reconciled. He was also worried that now my views about the

Church were out in the open I could be at risk of losing the children. After one of my calls Clive rang Black in the hope that, as two religious men, they could help us patch up our marriage. He told me Black was initially friendly and tried to win him over by saying there was always someone who was a problem in a Christian Church and I was that someone.

But when Clive replied that when a marriage breaks up it is never zero versus one hundred per cent, Black became quite aggressive. Clive told me that Black insisted it was entirely my fault and made outrageous allegations about me, saying that I was a thief, a spendthrift and rebellious, and had caused all kinds of trouble in the marriage. Calling me a thief apparently referred to the time I shoplifted jewellery from a gift shop when I was a difficult teenager.

I was terribly upset. Clive tried to reassure me and said he had never heard any minister talk in such a vindictive way about one of his congregants. Nor did he understand why Black seemed to be pushing us towards breaking up rather than helping to bring us together. But I knew he had behaved in similar ways with other couples going through difficulties. He often interfered and when one partner questioned his authority or disagreed with him, instead of helping the couple towards reconciliation, as one would expect from a religious leader, both he and Heather often advised separation at an early stage. He would even offer the support of the Church to assist the fight against the beleaguered partner. I couldn't understand why a pastor who appeared to be a firm defender of family values would want to be instrumental in the break-up of any marriage.

Nothing happened for a couple of weeks, but I noticed that my friends were keeping away from me. I had far fewer phone calls and no one asked me round for coffee or to join them on a social outing. I dreaded that what I had always feared was coming true – that if you dare take a stand against the Church you are quickly left on your own. I tried not to think about the loneliness for either me or the children. Then, on one of the longest days of the year, I was told Black wanted to take Peter and me out for lunch. Peter even took a day off work to come. This time we met at the Willow Tree, a popular restaurant on the road out of town. I took my two books on cults with me in a large handbag. When we arrived I was surprised to see that already seated at a large table were not only Black and Heather, but also a number of the most important people in the Church's hierarchy, the ones I used to call Black's cronies. I knew immediately I was in big trouble and felt very intimidated.

There was some small talk, then I was asked why I was withdrawing from God. Normally such a loaded question was the prelude to my breaking down in tears, but this time I was determined to be resolute and at one point pulled the two books out of my bag, threw them across the table towards Black, and said loudly, 'They are about cults and I want you to read them. Can they both be full of lies?' He remained very controlled and barely glanced at the books. Peter didn't say a word and I was angry that he didn't support me. The meal ended soon afterwards and about a week later Peter told me he had decided he wasn't going to leave the Church with me and that we would have to get a divorce, but I could have the house and the children.

We then got into a huge argument that went on and on. As 10 p.m. approached I suddenly felt so desperate to get away that I went up to each child's bedroom, gathered them up in my arms and put them in the car. Peter didn't attempt to stop me and I drove them round town until we came to one of its less prepossessing hotels, where I booked us all into a family room that I hoped wouldn't break the bank. As soon as they got into bed they fell asleep again and didn't wake until the morning. They thought it was great fun to wake up in a hotel room, and ate the sweets and drank the cans of Coca-Cola from the small fridge, neither of which they were allowed at home. I was so naive that I thought it was all thrown in with the cost of the room and I nearly fell over when I was given a bill for £120. I heard later that Peter and other Church members spent a lot of the night driving around trying to find me.

Paul and Rebecca told me they had heard our shouting match at home and had both got out of bed and sat on the stairs crying. Paul hated our argument and said no kid wants to hear their parents screaming at each other as they are a child's idols. He had eventually gone back to bed and put a pillow over his head to drown out the sound. I managed to get the children to school on time, and although Peter had gone to work when I got home, when he returned that evening we were calmer with each other. I knew that, even though I wanted him to come with us, I had to continue to prepare to leave with just the children if in the end he wouldn't. In the meantime I knew I shouldn't draw any attention to myself or be too argumentative as it could hamper my ability to copy the CDs. Although Wendy now had their passports and birth certificates, in my anxious state I didn't feel it would make the children any safer.

The best way to manage, I decided, was to put on a façade, pretend that everything was fine after all and submit quietly to my current life. It was easier to do in theory than in practice, and inevitably Peter and I became more distant from each other. We continued to sleep together but we didn't make love together nearly as often as we used to. My resolution fell apart on a Monday evening at the beginning of July after church. Peter was sitting at the kitchen table and suddenly said I mustn't keep hanging round with Kath, who had come on that critical visit to the bookshop with me, now she had left the Church. Someone must have seen us in the street together and reported back. Peter added that I must change our phone number so she couldn't contact me.

I replied that he couldn't tell me who I could and couldn't see. His response was a bombshell. He said that when we divorced he would get custody of the kids and I wouldn't get a penny. I was standing by the cooker drinking tea from a mug and I was so furious I threw it at him. It hit the wall behind him with such force that it left a dent. I shouted that I would get the kids. He was so angry that he rushed towards me with his fists clenched and, for a nasty moment that felt like ages, I was sure he would hit me. I fell to the ground and curled up into the foetal position to protect myself. Nothing happened and when I dared look up, I saw Daniel. He must have woken up and sneaked downstairs, and he was watching us.

I scrambled to my feet, put him back to bed, stumbled out of the house and into the car, drove to a phone box and called the police. I told them my husband had physically threatened me and they told me not to move from the phone box and that they were on their way. I had barely put the phone down when I thought that if the police got involved, so would social services, and I might lose the children. I left the phone box, drove to Kath and Robin's home, and knocked on the door. They gave me a little whisky to calm me down and I stayed the night with them.

First thing next morning I went to see my GP, who noted my extreme anxiety, suggested I contact the domestic abuse police officer at our local station, and said he was concerned for the safety of me and my children. When I got home Peter, his aunt and the four children – who were on holiday from school – were all there. Celia was cold and distant, and said Peter had told her about our row and that I, as his wife, should know that men occasionally hit their wives and I should take these things as a matter of course. I couldn't believe what I was hearing.

Peter, however, apologized to me and said he had made an appointment for us to see Black. We left the children with Celia and when we got to his office, Black, Heather and Charlotte were already there. Peter and I sat down on one of the leather sofas and Black sat opposite us. He said he had heard that Peter has been slapping me around and he began to laugh. I was speechless that anyone, let alone a religious leader, could think it funny when a man hit his wife. I should have known better than to expect sympathy and compassion.

'You are sick,' I blurted out, and at the same time realized in my heart that I had lost the battle to keep Peter with me.

* * *

On the surface this confrontation with Black had echoes of countless others I had had when I first arrived at the Church as a young teenager. The huge difference this time was that I no longer felt cowed by his presence. My conversations with Clive had helped me understand how abusive organizations and their leaders operate. During the conversation I thought to myself, 'Black is not, as I've believed for so long, God on earth. He is just a man.' It gave me the strength to stand my ground and argue with him.

As Black showed me neither sympathy nor understanding, when our meeting was over I followed my doctor's advice and contacted our local domestic abuse officer, WPC Howell. She asked if I wanted her to come round but I said I was OK, so instead she gave me her phone number in case I needed her in the future. I put it in a tiny red wallet that I called 'my secret number pouch', where I also kept the phone numbers for Clive and Wendy, and my phone card. For the next few weeks I felt I was living on a knife edge.

Peter, meanwhile, had rung Clive and asked to see him. Clive thought Peter was coming on his own and hoped we could begin to work our way towards reconciliation. Instead he turned up with a senior member of the Church and repeated Black's allegations about me, including the one that I was a spendthrift. Clive had studied our bank statements and asked Peter to give him examples. Peter complained about a £500 Smeg fridge I had bought. The purchase had in fact been a joint decision and we used some of the money Peter had been left by a relative. His priority had been to give a tenth of the legacy to the Church. Clive then asked if it was true that Peter had hit me and that Black had laughed about it. Peter said that it was, but that Black only laughed because he wanted to lighten the atmosphere between us.

Clive then asked how a Christian minister could make light of someone hitting a woman. By this time Peter was so angry that he and his ally from the Church stood up and stormed out. I don't quite know why they came to see Clive, except perhaps to try to alienate him from me. Things were by now snowballing so fast that at the beginning of August Wendy suggested I come to see her again. I needed another excuse to go to London and as a new dinosaur exhibition had just opened at the Natural History Museum I told Peter that I wanted to go and take the kids to see it. It was true in a way, but I still felt sneaky and nervous.

Black went to India at the beginning of that same month for another preaching tour and left instructions that Peter and I should go away for a weekend and try to sort out the marriage. I couldn't understand why, except that if I stayed, then so would the children, and he didn't want to lose four future members. Celia agreed to look after all the children and Peter booked a B & B in Norfolk. We spent a day in the Broads messing around in a boat, and in the evening we went out for a meal. I told Peter I couldn't carry on the way things were. He listened and later that night we made love, but overall it was a tense time.

Chapter 10

Escape

When we got back from our weekend away Carol came round to say she'd like to give a birthday party for me. It was both kind and brave of her. It was obvious that I was being ostracized but I think she wanted to make me feel loved. About sixty people were invited, all Tadford members apart from my parents. Carol organized a buffet of finger food, a cake with turquoise icing and some party poppers. As usual there was no alcohol. My birthday present from Peter was the new novel by Penny Vincenzi. It saddened me because I don't much like popular fiction, and he obviously hadn't made any effort, choosing the first book he'd seen on the display table at the local store.

The occasion was a nightmare from beginning to end. I was pleased my parents came but it was difficult for them. They knew the background and how anxious

I was but they had to keep their feelings hidden. The guests weren't very friendly and the atmosphere was strained. It didn't help that I was totally on edge in case some of my boxes of evidence were discovered. I had hidden them in our chaotic laundry room, along with some boxes of junk that we still had not got round to sorting out, and was scared that one of the guests might stumble across them as they wandered round our house.

A few days after the party one of the teachers rang to tell me Rebecca had had an accident during a netball match whilst jumping high for the ball. I rushed over to the school. Her right leg was at a strange angle to her body and it was clearly broken. I took her to the hospital, where an X-ray confirmed a nasty break. She was seen in quick succession by a house officer, a registrar and finally a consultant, before being taken to theatre for an operation, and her leg was put in plaster. Peter arrived and we agreed I would stay with Rebecca overnight and Celia would help look after Paul and the twins.

Rebecca was allowed home the following morning. Normally if a child was ill, friends would pop round with flowers, chocolates or a present for the child, but not one person turned up or even rang. I was ostracized. I had seen this sort of shunning before. Gossip always spread like wildfire within Tadford if someone was going against the Church. Even Carol and Celia kept away, which was very unusual. It hit me with a seismic jolt that they had all given up on me. I no longer counted. I was unacceptable. Unclean. Abandoned, not just by fellow members of the Church, but, in their eyes, also by God Himself. I felt panic-stricken. I had always dreaded this possibility and now it had become a reality. Part of me felt I might disintegrate on the spot. Collapse in a heap and beg for forgiveness.

Instead, by the time my first visitor arrived three days later, I felt a little stronger and more resolute. It was Olivia Porter. She didn't ring the front doorbell but came round to the back of the house and knocked on the laundry-room window. I was stacking some of our boxes of junk on top of the boxes of evidence to hide them more effectively and I nearly jumped out of my skin. I let her in through the kitchen door but I didn't want to sit down with her in case she started lecturing me. I first loaded the dishwasher, and then carried on energetically cleaning the kitchen as she talked.

She said that I was no longer the Sarah she knew and she was very worried that I had gone away from God. For the first time since I'd been at Tadford I managed to detach myself from her words. I realized what she was saying was merely emotional blackmail. She had told me something similar at the first conference my parents brought me to, when I was a teenager and had tried to walk out. Although it worked on me then, it didn't this time and I realized she could no longer manipulate me. She must have been aware of this too and didn't stay long.

Rebecca's accident was a turning point for me. I felt Tadford was no longer a proper environment in which to bring up my children. They hadn't mentioned anything about being ostracized at school, but I felt I could no longer trust the school to look after them and so I kept them all at home. Black was still in India when Rebecca's accident happened but was due back on the first Saturday of September. Peter went to see him soon after he returned, and then returned home. Although he refused to talk about what had happened between us, that night we made love on the sofa. On Sunday morning he left for Church with Paul, Luke and Daniel. Rebecca was still too poorly to go and I stayed at home with her. It was the anniversary of the day that Peter had asked me to marry him, but this time there wasn't much in the way of romance. I made our usual Sunday roast dinner, but Peter didn't eat or talk a great deal.

Afterwards he sat quietly in the kitchen just below the chip in the wall where I had thrown my mug of tea at him. All of a sudden the phone rang and made me jump. It was his uncle Patrick. After a few words with him, Peter hung up the phone and went upstairs. Minutes later he came down carrying his Bible and said he had to go to Tadford. It wasn't unusual, but suddenly I felt in my heart that this was the day it would all be over between us. While he was away my friend Barbara Harrison popped round. She was the first and only friend who had dared come. I told her she shouldn't stay, because she was bound to get into trouble. As soon as she left she was called into Black's office and told off.

Peter came back at 7 p.m. I tried to be civilized and suggested we have some Eccles cakes, our usual Sunday evening treat. 'Maybe,' he said. He then picked up his toolbox and wallet, and walked towards the front door. I asked, 'Where are you going?' 'Uncle Patrick's,' he replied. 'When are you coming back?' I asked. 'Never,' he replied, and walked off down the road.

It was a completely emotionless departure. He didn't say goodbye to me or the children. I instinctively double-locked the front door, then checked that all the windows were closed. I felt I was under siege, terrified in case one of the senior Church members broke in and took my children. I didn't tell them what was going on. I didn't want them to know our world had collapsed – not before I knew what was happening and had tried to put on a good front for them. It helped keep my own panic at bay. I put the children to bed as if nothing were wrong. Then at 9 p.m., when they were settled, I phoned my mother. I told her what had happened, trying to keep the hysteria out of my voice. I hadn't planned it this way.

In fact I hadn't really planned it in any way at all. I knew I had to leave, but I hadn't sorted out when or how.

I then rang Peter's aunt and uncle to check if he was coming home. Patrick answered the phone and said he wasn't. He then said the words I had been dreading to hear – that my marriage to Peter was over. All I could think of saying was that Peter didn't have any clothes and suggested I pack him a suitcase of what he might need. It was ridiculous really, and a clear sign I was in shock. Patrick agreed but said he wouldn't come into the house to collect it. In a daze I then neatly packed Peter's things, and sprayed everything lightly with my perfume, Rive Gauche. I have no idea why, except perhaps to show that in spite of everything I still loved him.

I felt confident Peter was being placed under enormous pressure by his aunt, his uncle and Black to make a choice between his own family and the Church, but I still clung to the receding hope that he would choose me and the children. I left the suitcase outside my locked front door and waited nervously inside until Patrick arrived by foot to collect it at 11.30 p.m.

Once the case had gone, the enormity of what had happened hit me like a door slamming in my face. I was now on my own. I desperately wanted Peter to come with me, but he had obviously chosen Tadford and God over his wife and family. He no longer belonged to me. But I couldn't change. Clive had helped open my eyes.

My moment had come, and I had no option but to stand my ground. There was nothing to keep me at Tadford. Nor were any of us safe. I had to protect my children, and that meant leaving as soon as I could.

Time was rushing by. At midnight I rang Clive and sobbed down the phone, 'He's left me.' He tried to calm me and agreed that I should get away without delay. He asked if my parents could come and be with me. I rang them again. It was the middle of the night but they answered immediately and agreed to leave once they had found someone to look after their cats and dog. It would take them at least five hours to reach me and until they did I had to stay awake.

Unknown to me, Dad immediately rang a Church of England vicar in town. He'd been talking to him about me for months, and now asked if a congregant of his could sit with me until they arrived. They needed to make sure I was safe and no one could take the children. The kindly vicar organized a rota of members who stayed with me throughout the day. I was edgy and agitated and still did not dare to go to sleep. I turned on the radio and for a while forced myself to dance to music to keep myself awake and occupied.

Then I started gathering what I thought I'd need. I was in such a state of shock I kept packing and unpacking things into bin bags for the children. Then I'd stop altogether and tidy up. I rang Dinah, explained briefly that I was leaving Tadford and Peter, and asked if I could leave some clothes in her garage. She didn't ask for any explanation. Perhaps she had heard Peter and me arguing when we lived next door. Thankfully, she immediately agreed. Her easy willingness to help was a life-saver.

My parents arrived in the afternoon. We all burst into tears and held each other tight. It was very emotional. They felt guilty and kept saying they were so sorry. I was crying all the time and telling them, 'I can't live this life anymore. I have to get out of here. I can't do it anymore.' Now that my parents were there, I explained in simple terms to the children that Daddy had left us and we had to go away. We couldn't stay at Tadford, I said, because it wasn't safe. I don't think they really understood what was going on.

When I'd filled a few bin bags, Dad and I carried them outside to put them in my trusty old Ford. It had gone. We both ran down the road to the Church and found it in the car park. I tried to start it, but the ignition didn't work. Dad suggested looking under the bonnet and when we did we found that the battery had been removed and was nowhere to be seen. I assumed that this was Peter's doing. We only had the one car and he certainly needed one to get to work, so I partially understood, but why he had been so sneaky about it and hadn't asked me whether he could keep it I've never found out. I burst into tears of rage. I didn't want to confront Peter so I rang the police instead. They said it was a domestic incident and wouldn't get involved. I had to leave the car there, which meant we couldn't travel in convoy as I'd hoped. We'd all have to pile into my father's Vauxhall Cavalier, and there would be much less room for our possessions. So I filled his car with my bulging bin bags and drove them to Dinah's, where I deposited them in her garage. I also left her our cat, Wilma, a beautiful tabby. There was sadly no room for her in the car and Dinah had always admired her. In a way giving her Wilma was my way of saying 'thank you' to Dinah, however odd it might sound.

We had also recently bought an eight-week-old Border collie, called Potter, and I couldn't leave him behind. We took him to the vet and he gave us tablets to make him sleep in the car. Every minute that passed made us all more anxious and we expected someone to challenge us or try to grab the children. Eventually we got to bed, by which time I was so exhausted I managed to sleep for a few hours. I knew we only had room for absolute essentials, but it seemed to take for ever to work out what we couldn't do without.

My parents' home would be too small for us all to stay in. Anyway, as the Church knew their address it would be too risky to keep the children there. I rang Kath, the friend who had come to the bookshop with me, and asked if we could stay with her for a couple of nights. She and Robin now lived in the west of England and had a holiday cottage close to their house. Luckily it was empty and she said we were welcome to use it.

In the end we set off on Tuesday evening. Everything happened in such a rush that I left with only £5 in my pocket. I have no idea how we managed to pile four kids, a drugged dog, a selection of bin bags and me into the back of Dad's car, but we did, with Luke on Rebecca's lap, Daniel on Paul's and me in the middle. All very illegal, but all very necessary.

I had been so preoccupied with the practical side of leaving that it was only when my father actually drove off that the implications of what I was doing suddenly hit me. I gasped at the magnitude of it all. I was going against what God wanted. He had selected me to be a member of Tadford. He had chosen my husband and now I was defying Him by running away. Fear turned my blood to ice as I waited to drop dead at any moment. Wave after wave of panic flooded through me. Would He also kill my innocent children? And what about my parents? Perhaps we would have a terrible crash. Perhaps a thunderbolt would descend from Heaven.

I thought I was rescuing my children and setting them free, but perhaps I was instead condemning them to their own destruction. I glanced at them on either side of me. They were sitting quietly, their eyelids heavy with sleep, four pictures of innocence without a care in the world.

I began to sob. Quietly, so as not to wake them, but from the bottom of my soul. I was too distraught to speak. I knew Mum was exhausted and didn't want to talk. Dad didn't talk either as he was concentrating on driving the overladen car. The combination of my fear and my physical and emotional exhaustion kept me weeping for hours. It all seemed so unreal and although crying usually releases tension, I dared not relax for a second as I expected each one to be my last.

Many hours after the sun had set we arrived at Kath and Robin's holiday cottage. Everything had been prepared for us, and it was warm and cosy. I couldn't believe it. Not only were we all still alive, but it had been a totally uneventful journey. I quickly settled the children, and then Mum and Dad turned round and started on their long drive up north. I slept for a few hours and woke up in the morning feeling a little more rested. I knew I had to move on, but the future was too frightening. Virtually all my decisions had been made for me at Tadford, but now I had to make every one myself. This included immediate major lifestyle choices, such as where to live and finding a school for the children. I was filled with fear. It didn't help that I had come away without any money apart from that fiver.

I also spent a lot of time trying to answer the children's questions. They mainly wanted to know where Daddy was and when were we going home. I tried to give them simple but honest answers without going into too much detail. How do you explain to children that where they have lived all their lives is actually a bad place? And that their Daddy has decided to stay there rather than be with them. Instead, I said we had come away so they would be safe and hopefully Daddy would join us very soon.

I talked endlessly to Kath, too. After a couple of days, when I felt a bit stronger, one of my parents' friends came to collect me and the children, and kindly drove us all north to my parents' home, which was many, many hours away. By chance she worked in the local authority housing department and explained where I had to go and what I had to do. She also mentioned how important it was to explain carefully what had happened to me.

Dad then drove me to the council's housing department, which was at the top of a bleak hill not far from where they lived. It was a grey, freezing-cold, windy day and as I climbed out of Dad's car with the children I thought, 'What am I doing in this God-forsaken place? I really haven't thought this through.' I had no idea where I was going or how I was going to live. All I knew was that I wanted to find somewhere fairly close by that didn't link me to Mum and Dad, and, as I had no car, it had to be close to a school.

I'd never been inside a social-services office and it was an alien experience. I hadn't a clue how the system worked. I also felt so ashamed. The office was grubby and when I was called by the female employee who was to help me, I went to pieces and burst into tears. The children were very upset at seeing me cry and Rebecca came over to me and held me tight.

Bless her heart, the adviser turned out to be an absolute star. She handed me some forms to fill out but quickly realized I was too distressed to do so and filled them out for me. She told me to go to a local letting agents and try to find a house, and explained that the council would pay for it. Dad drove us there and to my huge relief they said they had a four-bedroom house in the middle of a town about ten miles away that had just been renovated and sounded just right.

I rushed to see it and the moment I opened the door I felt enormously grateful. The Victorian terraced house was very clean and fully furnished, with a sweeping staircase that led up to its four bedrooms. The smallest bedroom, where I put the twins, had bunk beds, and the other two, for Paul and Rebecca, each had single beds. The house also had an old-fashioned pink bathroom, and a small kitchen and a large living area downstairs. It overlooked an old, derelict mill, but the view didn't matter, particularly as there was a courtyard and a raised garden area where the children could play. It felt safe as there were houses on either side and a doctor's surgery and a junior school across the road. What's more, we could move in immediately. I felt so lucky.

Dad kindly paid the deposit. He then drove me back to the social-services office and they confirmed that they would pay the rent. Mum managed to gather some bed linen from local church members and I moved in, thanking God I had somewhere to live. I then rang WPC Howell, the friendly officer who had helped me before I left, and she liaised with our local police to arrange discreet police protection. Officers weren't stationed outside the front door, but they were aware that there was a potential problem and knew to attend immediately if I dialled 999. It helped me feel a little more secure. Clive had wanted the children to go on the child-protection register but I disagreed, because I mistakenly thought it meant they could be taken away from me.

It was still my wish that we would stay together as a family, and once we had settled in I told the children that we must pray that God would bring Daddy to join us. Despite all that had happened I knew I still loved Peter. He was my husband and I felt we had grown up together, almost from childhood, to parent four special children. We were only halfway through life's journey.

So every evening they would ask God to take care of all the important people in their lives, but especially their Daddy.

Chapter 11

Starting Again

I kept the children home for a few days to help them settle and feel more secure. I also needed space to draw my breath. It seemed so odd to be without Peter and it was desperately sad to be making a new home on my own.

Because I'd had no practice at taking decisions or planning a strategy, my entire focus had been on getting away from Tadford. I didn't imagine anything beyond that. I now realized I'd been totally naive. The battle for my life was just beginning and I didn't have the skills I needed.

I found everything in my new life hard to deal with. I was physically exhausted from the trauma of leaving my home and Peter, so on a purely practical level I found it difficult to look after four needy children. I was also too emotionally drained to think straight and, after so many years in a rigid, controlled environment, psychologically almost incapable of making decisions. Each decision, whether big or small, seemed like a huge mountain to climb. I regularly rang Clive for advice, but although he wanted to help me, he was wise enough to know how important it was for me to learn to rely on myself as soon as possible.

Looking back, I can see how well he dealt with me. If I asked him what to do about something, he would reply with an open question to try to encourage me to make my own choice. For example, if I was worried about what activity to do with the children, rather than say, 'Why not take them for a walk in the country?' he'd say, 'Would you prefer to take the children for a walk in the country, to the local animal park or for a milkshake in a café?'

He'd also ask me what I thought the effect of any decision might be, which was a good way of helping me think it through. Practical decisions I found the least difficult and emotional ones the hardest.

I was used to running a home and doing the cooking, so I just about managed to get the children up for break-fast and bathed and in bed at night. But our days had been planned round when Peter would be home and it seemed so strange to be on my own. I felt particularly lonely sleeping in a double bed by myself. Sometimes I placed pillows horizontally beside me so that it felt as if

Peter were there. I discovered I'd taken by mistake one of Peter's photo albums with pictures of him as a child, and I used to sit and look through it endlessly. Later I returned it to Celia.

After those few crucial days I enrolled the children at school, just across the road. It was important for them to return to some sort of normality as soon as possible, to give them stability and a routine. The school had a uniform and I got an allowance to pay for it from social services.

I told the headmaster in general terms what had happened to us. It wasn't necessary to be too precise. I also made the point that no one was to collect my children from school apart from my parents and me.

The first few weeks were understandably traumatic for them as well as for me. They had left their home and their father, and the new school was so very different from what they had been used to that, more than anything, it underlined the enormity of what I had done. There had been only about eight pupils per class at Tadford, but at their new school it was more in the region of thirty-five, and understandably the classes seemed enormous and unwieldy to my children. The work was much less demanding compared with what they had had to do at Tadford, which was helpful at this early stage. The real problem was that none of them could cope with the way the school operated. At Tadford they had been given no options about what they did, but now they often had to choose between as many as four or five activities and none of them knew how to respond. They even found it difficult to decide whether to choose a pen or a pencil to draw with.

At Tadford all lessons had taken place in total silence, with each child working alone, but now the children often worked in groups and chatted together about what they were doing. All of my children had no idea how to manage and found the noise level very stressful. Luke was so anxious he became hysterical each morning as we reached the school gates, and clung tightly to me. He had to be peeled off by a teacher and I could hear his screams as I left, which was very upsetting both for me and for Daniel, who despite always being the stronger of the twins, was fragile in his own way too. This routine lasted months but the teachers reassured me that he calmed down once he was in the classroom. But I knew he was very unhappy and missed his Daddy and his friends.

Although Rebecca would walk into school without a fuss, she didn't fit in at all. She'd become very religious and the teachers expressed concern that she preached to the children about Jesus and kept telling them that if they didn't behave God would strike them down. She was merely parroting what she had learned at church, but I could understand how disturbing it must have been for both the staff and pupils. Some of the girls would ask her what she was 'on about', but she couldn't explain, so they began picking on her.

She also suffered when her teacher raised her voice, even when it was merely to get attention rather than to tell anyone off. When her teacher at Tadford School had shouted, it was a prelude to her being 'whacked', so when her new class teacher spoke loudly Rebecca automatically put her hands over her head to protect herself. It was all a terrible struggle for her. She felt completely out of her depth in this new world and among so many different people, and very soon she became a permanently angry little girl. Although Tadford School was awful in many ways, it was what she knew and all the children, her included, were polite and well behaved. She couldn't understand why these qualities weren't valued in her new school. Instead she was bullied and couldn't make friends. She remembers one child in her class sticking up two fingers at her. She had no idea what it meant but in turn stuck up two fingers just as the teacher looked at her. She was immediately taken in front of the headmaster and told off, but she had no idea what she had done wrong until the head explained.

It was all too different from what she had been used to and she got into lots of fights, both at school and at home. Paul could wind her up in seconds and if she had no one to fight she'd sometimes punch walls or trash her bedroom. She was quick-tempered, had a short attention span and was stressed all the time.

Paul also struggled to cope and said he found it 'weird' to be able to choose what he wanted to do. He reacted by becoming very quiet and withdrawing into himself. In one way his response caused the least problems, but I recognized how unhappy he was and gave him a piece of blanket, which had originally been a cot duvet, to help comfort him. He called it 'softie' and soon wouldn't go anywhere without it. Most of the time he also carried a soft toy squirrel around with him.

His other key problem was me, and this I found considerably harder to deal with. He worried about how I was and didn't know what to do when he saw me upset. He knew how much I missed Peter and felt that somehow he had to be the man in the house and look after all of us, now that Daddy was no longer with us. He often slept in my bed, hugged me when I cried and always tried to be around to keep me company. Paul was the most sensitive of the children to my mood and the truth was he had every cause to worry. I was in shock, and although I tried to stay strong for them, because they were going through so much, I felt lonely, isolated and frightened myself, and it was very difficult not to let some of that show. I never got irritable with them, but they saw me cry far too often.

I found it difficult to relate to the other mothers at the school gate. Some of them seemed very nice but I didn't know what to say to people I had been told for so many years that they were of the devil and part of an evil world. I now felt I fitted into neither the normal world nor the Christian world.

I was also desperately worried about money. Wendy wrote to Peter as soon as I left our home to ask for maintenance. She also requested that he pay for the children to be put into private schools because that is what they had been used to, but he refused to consider it and in the first months of separation paid maintenance, although spasmodically. When the money didn't arrive I tried to survive on benefits of £80 for two weeks plus child allowance.

When my thoughts weren't focused on the children they usually turned to Peter. Less than a month after we parted, I sent him a letter expressing both my feelings for him and my anxieties over money. Wendy told me to be careful about what I wrote in case the contents were used against me, so I faxed it to her first.

I wrote:

Dear Peter

I trust you are OK after all that's gone on. I'd like you to know that I miss you, and so do the children. I'm writing to say that I've been thinking about Clive's advice and our marriage and everything, and although I hope that we can still be together at some

*point in the future, I think his idea that we do not see
each other for a while is a good one.*

*What is most important in all of this is the welfare
of the children. I don't need to tell you that, I'm sure.
But if you don't want to support them financially I'm
afraid that I will have to make an application to the
child support agency, as well as instructing my
solicitor to seek financial help.*

*Given the central place of our children in what has
happened, and in what is going to happen, it would
be really great if you could arrange, through Clive, to
get in touch with them. That doesn't mean that you
have to have anything to do with me, although we do
need to sort out our financial affairs. Could you
arrange a meeting with Walter to go through what
needs to be done, particularly with regard to standing
orders and direct debits? We discussed this when we
were with Clive and I'm sure you know what I
consider to be the right way forward.*

*Just a few words about the children: they're all fine,
and they're still being brought up and educated in a
good Christian way, although everything's very
different to how it was at Tadford. They often speak
about you and when they do it brings a tear to my eye.*

I will always love you Peter.
In peace,
Sarah xxxx

He didn't reply but I continued to live in hope that he might leave Tadford and over time sent him further loving letters. It was hard to do because each time he failed to reply I felt a further rejection.

Despite the sentiments in my letter I initially felt very cross with God for putting me through such a trauma and not letting Peter leave with me. What had I done to deserve being alone and lonely? I had been a devoted Christian for so many years and when I needed Him most He wasn't there. Why didn't He answer my prayers and let Peter leave with me? Despite my anger I decided I would take the children to church as I wanted them to have a Christian upbringing. I initially chose the local Charismatic church, but it was a disaster. Many of the songs were so familiar I became very upset and couldn't cope with it, so we all left.

I became so reclusive that I walked about with my head down to try to make myself as invisible as possible. The town where we lived was, however, such a small community that the locals couldn't have missed the arrival of a stranger with four children, especially as we were so inappropriately dressed.

My children hadn't worn casual clothes at Tadford so I had none to bring. Instead they all looked like little adults going to a wedding. My old-fashioned, formal clothes were equally unsuitable for living in the countryside. But I couldn't afford to buy different clothes, so we all had to make do.

After about three months, thanks largely to Clive's help, I began to feel that I had both the right and the ability to make up my own mind. This was rather over-optimistic, but I did at least manage to take two crucial decisions. One was that I must stay strong for the children. The second was that if I wasn't going to be destroyed by what had happened to me I had to force myself to accept it and move on. I could only cope with life day by day, but whenever I cried I tried to do something positive afterwards so I could console myself that at least I was taking tiny steps forward.

For example, when I lived with Peter, I would feed the children at about 5.30 p.m., then get them bathed and in bed before he was home so we could eat together. Now it would have been both pointless and sad to eat on my own, so I gave them snacks when they got in from school and later we had a cooked meal as a family. I found Saturday nights particularly difficult once the children were in bed as there was no one to sit and chat to.

As the shock of my departure slowly dimmed and I felt more settled in my new home, in common with many women I decided to mark a new stage in my life by a change of hairstyle and so I put some highlights in. At Tadford I had not been allowed to colour my hair and I hoped it would not only make me look more attractive but also help put the past behind me.

I also began chatting to a neighbour, who turned out to be a single parent like me. After about six months he invited me to go with him to the local pub. At first I didn't know how to respond. I had no idea how to cope in what to most people was a normal social situation. I had been indoctrinated to believe that pubs were dens of iniquity and Christians mustn't go inside. I thought about it for days and, having finally decided to give it a try, arranged for my parents to babysit the children.

I didn't enjoy it and felt a total outsider. My neighbour introduced me to some of the regulars, but I found conversation extremely difficult. We didn't have any reference points in common. I'd barely watched television, hadn't been to the cinema since I was a teenager and had long stopped listening to pop music, so I couldn't join in when everyone was chatting about popular culture.

There was also an extremely embarrassing moment when one of the men mentioned the word 'vice'. The only vice I knew was the one my father had in his shed, which didn't fit in with what he was saying. I asked him to explain what he meant and when he did I felt incredibly naive and stupid. It was a long time before I could face going to a pub again and the experience emphasized how much I had missed and what a difficult journey it was going to be to feel relaxed and have something in common with people who lived normal lives.

In some ways it was rather like being a teenager again while everyone around me was grown-up. My next social foray was with the very nice mother of one of the boys in Luke and Daniel's class. She was naturally sociable and when I told her the basic facts about my life in a strict church she insisted I experience a night out at a nightclub. My parents babysat again and we went to a club not far from where we lived. Once again I found the experience very difficult. I loved the music, but didn't like the way men sized women up as if we were pieces of meat in a factory. I couldn't cope with people swearing or being physically intimate in public. And as I hadn't heard the music before I couldn't sing along with it like everyone else. I also struggled to do the right dance movements, which were totally foreign to me. All in all, I realized that this type of entertainment wasn't for me.

I did, though, indulge in a small act of defiance by smoking my first cigarette since I was a teenager. I felt like a naughty schoolgirl, but after trying one I took my own decision not to smoke again. My biggest achievement at the time was making the firm resolution to change the way I had been bringing up the children. I hadn't smacked them since we left Tadford and this alone had a major effect.

The first time Rebecca wet the bed after we left our home, she woke up in a terrible state and in between floods of tears cried, 'I am so sorry, Mummy, please don't smack me.' I held her tight and said, 'You are not going to be smacked again. Ever. It is not a problem if you wet the bed. I shall just change the sheets.' Once she and the twins knew they would not be hit they steadily improved and after a few months they stopped bedwetting altogether.

I also changed my attitude to what they ate. Meals at Tadford had always been regimented, with no choice, and the children were not allowed to have snacks. Now I told them that as long as they ate a proper cooked dinner in the evening, they could help themselves to whatever else they wanted at any time, provided it was healthy. I wanted them to feel able to leave food and have a choice. The three boys ate marvellously, but Rebecca had lots of issues with food.

In addition I rented a television and Paul in particular was amazed when he first saw *The Simpsons*. I also let them listen to any music of their choice. I used to watch television with them when I could and discovered that certain programmes made good topics of conversation with mothers at the school. But I continued to find it difficult to talk to them and kept getting the balance wrong. I was either too open and trusting, or, partly because I was used to a black-and-white world, too opinionated. Nor could I stand up for myself if someone disagreed with me. All in all, it was a very difficult mixture.

The best and entirely positive change to my children's lives was getting to know my parents. As they had met them only occasionally, it was Peter's aunt and uncle whom they thought of as their grandparents. I was delighted to see them gradually building a bond and Rebecca developed a particular attachment to my father, who became her male role model.

All our lives brightened up hugely when my sister Kerry rang and offered to pay for me, the children, and Mum and Dad to fly over to join her in Canada for Christmas. She was now married and living on the east coast with her husband Paul and their two children, Carla and Inigo. They were similar ages to Rebecca and the twins, but they had all met only once before, while we were still at Tadford.

The holiday was to be divided between Kerry's home and the nearby wintry mountains. She even offered to pay for skiing lessons for the children and said she had so many spare items of ski clothing that we didn't need to buy a thing. It was wonderfully generous of her and I was thrilled to accept. My lawyer Wendy informed Peter about the trip and I had to sign a guarantee that I would bring the children back on a set date. I then suggested to Wendy that perhaps Peter could meet them before

Christmas. I was keen that they maintain contact with their father and I'd been disappointed that he had not made any attempt to see them since we left Tadford.

After a lot of to-ing and fro-ing between lawyers we all met up at a restaurant near the airport just before our flight. It was rather awkward. Peter gave each of the children a Christmas present but, disappointingly, didn't stay long. Luckily they were so excited about the holiday that they were easily diverted. It was the first time any of them had flown and they loved looking out of the plane window. When we landed we took a bus for the forty-minute ride to Kerry's home and she picked us up from the bus stop. We stayed at the large family bungalow for four days so we could all get over any jet lag. Kerry also took us to some factory outlets where I bought some really cheap tracksuit trousers and lots of T-shirts for the children and myself, which made us look more normal in our country surroundings. We then went off to the mountains. Kerry had booked a large chalet for us all and we spent Christmas Day under crystal-clear skies and in temperatures of –10°C.

The children were brilliant at skiing, but it petrified me, so I stayed on the nursery slopes. I loved talking with Kerry, and the cousins all got on wonderfully well. It was so relaxing and the perfect escape. Just every now and then my thoughts would wonder about what might happen next in my life.

Just after New Year I rang Wendy to check if there was any news and she told me Peter had issued divorce proceedings. I was devastated. I knew from experience that when Tadford couples separated, a divorce was always sped through, but I hoped Peter might have missed me so much he would leave Tadford too. I knew in the back of my mind that whoever stayed behind was married off quickly to someone else, but I couldn't bear to take that thought on board.

It was particularly hard as I still had a strong faith. This ruled out divorce unless there was a compelling reason such as adultery, and I couldn't understand how Peter, whom I thought shared my views about divorce, could behave so differently. I believed our marriage had been for life. After all, I had basically only left him because I could no longer cope with the way we were controlled by Tadford. Although he had at times been brutal to me and the children, I believed that this was because he was trying to conform to how the Church decreed he should behave. I had assumed that when we left our home, he would have been so shocked that he would want to compromise. Instead, he had brutally cut me away. I felt so desolate and I don't know what I would have done without my family around me.

Peter's grounds for divorce was my unreasonable behaviour during our marriage. I wanted to counter-sue because I didn't think it was fair to blame me entirely for the marital breakdown, but Wendy advised me not to and said it didn't make much difference who divorced whom.

Once the holiday was over and I returned home with the children, the reality of my new life as a single mum really sank in. In the cold light of day I realized that this wasn't going to be a temporary change. It was how my life would be for the foreseeable future. Before I left Tadford I had never slept on my own without another adult in the house. I mourned the death of my marriage, the loss of my husband and my marital home, and began waking up with a start in the early hours. I worried about being totally responsible for the children's safety and well-being, and how vulnerable they were to being kidnapped. Both Clive and Wendy had warned me this was a serious concern, and when Clive told me that Black was accusing me of being psychologically unstable I sensed that would be the pretext for trying to get custody of my children.

I felt sure Black's view would be that Peter was spiritual while I was going to Hell and therefore was not competent to bring up the children. That was enough for them to try to take my children away and keep them hidden away from the courts until they could gather enough evidence to use against me.

A week after we returned from holiday my fears seemed justified. My friend Kath's husband Robin rang me late one night to say he'd met some people from Tadford who had casually mentioned that two men from the Church were coming up north to try to find me. He also reminded me that my parents' address was known to them.

At the time Mum and I had made an arrangement that we would take it in turns to make Sunday lunch and it was her turn the following day. I rang her so that she and Dad came to me instead, and they also agreed to stay overnight. I didn't talk to the children about my concerns, because they were too young to understand, but I think they all picked up on my anxiety. It particularly affected Luke, and from that time, despite Daniel's opposition to the idea, he would sleep only with the light on and the bedroom door open. He remained frightened of Black and worried that he might come to take him away.

When my parents returned home the next day, their neighbours told them that two men had turned up, rung the doorbell and looked through the windows of their house. I assumed they were from Tadford, although I couldn't know for certain. I was scared stiff and told the school to be particularly vigilant.

Chapter 12

A Roller-coaster Ride

As the weeks passed and nothing happened I slowly began to relax although I knew I would always have a nagging anxiety that my children could be taken away at any time. Over the weeks that followed, this feeling grew in intensity, and once it became unbearable I rang Clive, Wendy and my parents in quick succession and they all felt that, all things considered, it would be wise to move. I felt incredibly nervous of staying in the same town and immediately trawled through our local paper for a vacant property. Two days later I found a house about ten miles away. It was about the same size as our current home but when I went to see it I didn't think it had a good feeling. In one cupboard under the stairs I found what looked like a piece of old carpet, but when I bent down to move it I discovered that it was in fact several dead rats.

Call me evil, let me go

The place gave me the creeps but I thought I'd be able to sort out any rat problem and so we moved in. Mum and Dad organized about twenty people from their church – the same one I'd walked out of because the singing reminded me too much of Tadford – to come round with buckets of paint and they redecorated the entire house. It was incredibly kind of them. Unlike our last house, this one was unfurnished. I had no furniture, carpets, bedding, or even cutlery or crockery, so Wendy tried to get Peter to let me have some possessions from the family home. He refused. I was so short of money that in the end I went to a local auction to buy old furniture and beds.

It was only once we'd settled in that I realized that in my panic my decision to move had been made too fast. I don't know what might have happened if we had stayed, but our last house had become an oasis for us and we loved living there. It showed me that although I had made progress with my decision-making, moving house was too big a decision for me to take at the time. I suffered the consequences because we were now miles from the nearest shop, there was no bus service and the children would have to change schools. Nor was the rat problem easily sorted out. Although the local vermin agent came round regularly I still heard rats scurrying about at night. Once, when I went to comfort Luke after he'd had a bad dream, I saw several of them eating his toys. I grabbed him and for the rest of our time at our new house he slept with me. At least this meant that Daniel could once again sleep without the light being on in his room.

Unfortunately even the local school was not within walking distance and I had to buy a very old people carrier in which to ferry the children back and forth. It was on its last legs and the back doors wouldn't open because the locks were broken, so all of the children had to pile in through the front doors. The house was in such a rural setting that we were sometimes delayed in the morning by sheep, cows or hounds from the local hunt blocking the road.

Luckily, changing schools proved to be an excellent move. Luke made a really good friend and stopped crying every morning when I left him. The head teacher was wonderful too. He was also a Christian and could understand the children's background.

Unfortunately my own mood was still going up and down. Some days I felt positive and that I could cope with my new life. At other times I would wake up in the early hours weeping and feel near to despair. On one occasion I felt so dreadful that I called the Samaritans and within minutes the man on the line had me laughing. I was so grateful.

A few days after this, just as I was turning off the lights downstairs before going to bed, a large 4x4 drew up at the end of our drive and two men sat inside with the engine running and the lights on. Our house was down a single-track lane and so out of the way you couldn't mistakenly drive to it. The only reason to be there was to come to the house. I grew increasingly nervous as I watched them from the sitting room, especially as Potter was barking wildly throughout, but after about half an hour they drove off. I have no idea where they were from but I felt threatened, and I was terrified for my children.

I had asked Peter several times to send us some of the children's toys, books and bedding that I had left behind, but nothing arrived, so six months after I left him, I decided to take matters into my own hands. It was no more Mrs Nice Guy. I had had enough. My children were innocents in our separation and entitled to their things. Also the house was officially still partly mine. I looked in the local paper, phoned a man with a white van, and asked him how much he would charge to drive me down south and back, leaving at 4 a.m. He said £200. I then rang two men who I knew had fallen out with Black and asked them to meet me at 10 a.m. at my former marital home. I explained that I wanted them to help me pack the van with our things and then drive back up north.

I also asked a local police officer what to do to get protection in case it ended in a fight. He told me to go to the local police station and ask for officers to prevent a breach of the peace. My parents came to look after the children, and the van driver and I set off. All the way down I practised the exact phrase I had to use at the police station so I got it right. When we arrived I felt a mixture of anger and fear. I went into the police station and explained I was still a legal owner of my house and had to go inside to get some stuff but that my husband could be violent, so could I have a police officer to prevent a breach of the peace. They gave me four, saying one or two wouldn't be enough if Tadford was involved, and two police cars followed us to my former home.

I had worked out that Peter would have changed the back but not the front door locks. Just before I left he had put a new and very expensive door on the front of the house. Changing that lock would have been extremely costly and I guessed he would leave it. I was right. I let myself into the house through the front door and let the two men who had come to help me in through the back door. I showed them what I wanted to take and thought I was being very fair. The police stood on guard outside the house.

After a short while Peter's uncle came running across the field at the back of the house and came straight in through the back door, which I had mistakenly left unlocked. Someone must have telephoned him to tell him what was happening. He asked what was going on and I replied that it was my house as much as Peter's, which meant I had a right to some of our possessions. He then threatened me with the police. I responded that there was no need to call them, that he could go outside and talk to them himself. I then opened the front door and he approached one of the policemen. Once he had stepped over the threshold he wasn't allowed back into the house again. One of the policemen then asked to speak to me and questioned if it really was my house, as he had been told that it belonged to the Church. I rang my lawyer and she confirmed to him that it was owned by both Peter and myself, and the police were happy with that.

By this time ten or so members of the Church had arrived and stood around watching me. One of them wrote down everything that was being taken into the van while another took photographs. As they weren't allowed into the house they stood on the drive. It was very intimidating, particularly as I was running around like a headless chicken to get everything finished. I took lots of the children's toys and clothes, their bikes, bedding and one white leather sofa – but left the other one for Peter – all of my china, which I wrapped in duvets, and the dining table and six chairs.

When I had completed what I had come to do, I thanked the police and we left safely. I arrived back home in the late afternoon and unloaded all the things.

The children were thrilled to have their bikes, and rode up and down outside the house. I was absolutely shattered but pleased I had managed such a complex operation. My exhaustion lasted for weeks and I think it was the accumulation of so much that had happened to me. I would take the children to school, then come home and sleep nearly all day until I had to collect them in mid-afternoon. After about three days I would feel better, then the tiredness would overwhelm me again and I'd be almost out of action. It was a process I had to go through. Gradually, after a few weeks, I began to feel better and strong enough to get on with my new life.

I decided to start by going to the local Church of England church, which I thought would be easier for me than a Charismatic church, partly because the songs are so different. I wrote to tell Peter what I was doing because I wanted him to know I hadn't forsaken religion. Nor had I yet totally given up on his joining us, but I knew it wouldn't happen unless I somehow convinced him to see Tadford as I now did. When the children went to bed I did a lot of thinking. I knew several people who had left Tadford in dramatic and traumatic circumstances but had found it so difficult to pick up the pieces of their broken lives that they did nothing about the Church itself. I wanted to do something so that people would know what really went on there and how unjust much of it was.

Gradually a plan formed in my mind. I thought that if I could interest my local TV network to feature a brief story about me and my ordeal at Tadford on their news round-up after the national news, then what my children and I had endured there would not have been totally in vain. Word of it would surely eventually get back to Tadford. I rang the TV station, spoke to a senior executive and sent him a couple of Black's 'miracle' CDs to listen to first. At the very least, it would secure my children's safety as I thought – or perhaps just hoped – that no one would dare kidnap them when Tadford was under a media spotlight, however brief and dim it might be. I anticipated that it might also convince Peter to join us. In addition, I wanted to prove to Black that I had survived. After a desultory meeting on a rainy midweek day in an anonymous city-centre tower block, the executive told me that he didn't really think my story about goings-on in a church down south would be of sufficient interest to a northern audience. I was naturally disappointed, but at least I felt that I had tried to do something positive.

Several weeks later my lawyer rang to tell me that Peter had decided to seek custody of the children. I felt as if I had been punched in the stomach. My children meant everything to me and being a mother was my proudest achievement. I thought back to my decision to leave Tadford and felt that however painful uprooting us all had been, I had done the right thing. I wanted them to have freedom of choice, minds of their own and to be able to take decisions without having to ask someone. Nor did I want them to feel that God was a God of wrath waiting to strike them down at any moment.

This gave me strength and, although in my emotional turmoil I felt sure Peter stood a good chance of succeeding in his custody claim, I decided I would do everything I could to keep the children with me. Although I was penniless, while he had money and could give them a private education and a nice home, I took some comfort when my lawyer assured me she would work extremely hard on my behalf to keep them with me.

My custody case was scheduled to be heard at the end of March the following year. The day before I was due to appear Mum moved in to look after the children and Dad, who came along to keep me company, and I caught the overnight coach because it was cheaper than going by train. I was wearing a dark-blue suit from Next that I'd often worn for church at Tadford. We left home in the early hours of the morning and arrived at the court just after dawn. I didn't sleep a wink on the journey. I felt certain the Church would help Peter get a top barrister and was worried in case Black turned up because I knew how easily he won people round on first impressions. I felt my whole life was in the hands of one man, the judge. I didn't know how I would survive if he decided to take my children away from me and give Peter custody.

Black was there but didn't utter a word during the hearing. The proceedings didn't take long as the case was adjourned. A few days later Wendy was informed that Peter had dropped the case – I never found out why – and had agreed to hand all care of the children over to me. I felt extremely relieved, very emotional and so grateful that I had won such an important battle. It was agreed that Peter could visit the children up north, but a court order was drawn up to prevent them being brought into contact with any members of Tadford.

Sadly, Peter and I were divorced in June and a couple of months later I heard he had married another member of the Church. Although I suspected this would happen, the reality was difficult to cope with. All the children were upset but Rebecca was the most shocked. She tried to comfort me by saying she felt sure her father was more interested in rowing machines than women and blamed Black for pairing him off so quickly.

I knew how important it was for the children to keep in touch with their father, but Peter came to see them only once or twice a year. Initially, he refused to see me, so I would drop the children off at my parents' house, and he would collect them and bring them back from there. At least when he came to see them he did lovely things, like take them up to the moors for the day, fly their kites and then on to a café for lunch. The children said that now he was away from Tadford he was really cool and they particularly loved the time he took them to a steam-engine rally. Paul and the twins particularly loved it when he did what they called 'action man things', like taking them yachting on nearby lakes.

The trouble was, they said, that they had just got used to being with him and having a great time when he would go off again and they wouldn't see him for months, if not a whole year. Between when I left Tadford and the time when the financial settlement was sorted, they saw him only a handful of times. All four children blamed Black for this rather than their father.

Peter and I also had to sort out the financial settlement in a separate sitting of the court. I was dreading it and it was an arduous task to provide minute details of how much I spent each month on utility and food bills, petrol and even the children's school dinners.

Peter's lawyers disputed the amounts and the details of the arrangement went back and forth. We finally settled in October and agreed to split our assets, with the larger share going to me. Peter would now pay me a fixed monthly sum for maintenance and I would also get a substantial amount from the value of our house.

While the financial settlement was going on I went to the Charity Commission, which keeps records of all approved charities and their finances. I looked at the

Church's finances over a number of years and was shocked to see by how much they had increased over the period concerned. I wondered how much of this was as a result of members' donations.

The financial details of Tadford School also shocked me. Many of us had worked for nothing at the school, but now I saw that it spent a nominal sum on books while Black was taking a substantial five-figure annual salary as head. He seemed to me to be incredibly wealthy through the hard work and generosity of his congregation. Not only did he have a salary as head of the school, he earned money from his position in the Church, and no doubt also from Holy Bloom.

As soon as the financial settlement was sorted I tried to buy my own home. I contacted the local estate agents and one of them offered me a beautiful white detached house up on the moors. It had four double bedrooms and a single, a huge kitchen and a lovely garden with expansive views. On one side of the garden, behind a long screen of conifers, there was a small one-bedroom cottage, which I thought I could rent out. It was just within my price range and I put down the money I had been awarded by the court. I managed to get a mortgage and my sister Kerry loaned me a further sum, which I later repaid.

Everything was completed very quickly and we moved in by the beginning of December. Although it was our third move in just over a year it was wonderful to have our own home again but there was a sad finality that Peter wasn't sharing it with us. Once we had settled in I advertised the cottage as a self-catering let for holidaymakers and, to my delight, had several bookings. I felt that at last my life was moving forward and on this occasion felt grateful to God that He had looked after me and helped me buy my own home.

The house was close enough to the previous one that I didn't have to disrupt the children again by changing schools. Although Paul and the twins were getting on much better, unfortunately Rebecca's behaviour continued to deteriorate. She remained unable to relate to other children and couldn't cope with noise in the classroom. She still felt under threat when a teacher shouted and in response would shout, cry and even push desks over. She fought with the other girls too, and they picked on her, partly I suspect because she continued to spout religion.

She was becoming increasingly aggressive at home, too. When we got back from school she would throw things across the room and scream and shout. I was so worried about her that I took her to the local GP, who sent her for various tests, including one to see if she had a brain tumour. When all the physical tests came back negative, he then made an appointment for her to see a consultant child psychiatrist from the local Child and Adolescent Mental Health Service (CAMHS), who saw her during school hours. He was brilliant and soon diagnosed post-traumatic stress disorder. She was treated with individual psychotherapy, and medication was considered but not prescribed at this time.

The school head came up with the idea of breaking Rebecca's lessons down into fifteen-minute sections and after each section she was given a sticker for good behaviour or finishing her work. She was also allowed to leave the classroom whenever she felt she couldn't cope, and go to the head's office to sit quietly. It all worked very well and she began to steadily improve. If it wasn't for that head I don't know what would have happened.

Although Rebecca was still difficult, having my own home made me feel more stable and I gradually began to think about a career. I went through various options and decided on my original choice of social work. Black had stopped me trying to study when I was 18 and I wanted to prove to myself that I could do it. One of the few benefits of being at Tadford was that the Church was full of very committed people who worked long and hard. As a result I too had developed a strong work ethic and wanted to make my mark professionally in the world.

I sent off an application to the local university, where by a stroke of fortune there was a course running in social work, and to my delight I was accepted to start my course in September. I felt positive about the future and was delighted when my mother suggested she and Dad come over to our house for the August Bank Holiday and bring along my first cousin, Joy, who was the adopted child of my mother's brother, Uncle Arthur, and his wife, Auntie Eileen. I hadn't seen Joy during my years at Tadford and was keen to get back in touch. She came with a friend of hers from work who was temporarily living with her, called Stephen. His 6-year-old daughter, Ruth, had come earlier in the day with Joy and her two boys. Stephen was only a month younger than me, and we immediately hit it off and chatted happily for hours. He told me he was divorced and that Ruth lived with his ex-wife. He explained that he was lodging with Joy as he hadn't yet found anywhere to live and was working as a financial adviser in the same office as Joy.

Stephen seemed great fun and rang me a couple of days after he left, asking if he could come back the following weekend with Ruth. I agreed. That weekend went well too, although Luke told me he didn't like him. Stephen then asked if he could move in with me and did so three weeks later. It was ridiculously fast and I should have said no. But I was lonely, he was big in personality although slight in physique, and I think I viewed him as some sort of protector. I could have made a load of excuses, including 'I don't want to go any further with this relationship' or 'Can we take our time as I have come out of a very delicate situation?' but I didn't or couldn't. It's very difficult, when you have been undermined and ordered what to do and what to think for years, to find the confidence to stand firm.

I also started my social-work course, loved the work and, despite an initial academic struggle, I soon got into the swing of it and felt proud that I was keeping up with the other students. The New Year came and went and then it was Valentine's Day and my parents joined us. I was busy in the kitchen during the evening and when I walked into the sitting room Stephen opened the curtains to reveal my four children and Ruth holding up a large poster saying: 'Will You Marry Me?'

It had never crossed my mind that he would propose so soon into our relationship and I instinctively felt very awkward. By doing it in front of the family he had put me on the spot. Yet again I didn't have the courage to say no in front of everyone, so I said yes instead, and carried on with my work and concentrating on the children. The head of Rebecca's school was worried about her now she was ready to go to senior school because the local comprehensive was vast, with 1,300 pupils. Paul was already there and finding it hard to cope, and I agreed that it would be a disaster for Rebecca. Another, smaller comprehensive with a respected Special Needs unit seemed a better bet. The only problem was that it was much further away from home.

I decided to take Rebecca for an interview and they agreed to accept her as a pupil. I also managed to get funding from the council for her bus fare. She settled in well without any behaviour problems but the long journey, particularly as winter approached, became increasingly difficult for her. Although I hadn't wanted to move the other three children, in the end I decided there was no alternative. Rebecca's school agreed to take Paul and I found a junior school for the twins. What this all meant, however, was that we really had to move home, even though I'd have a much further commute to reach my university.

I easily sold my house and subsequently bought a 300-year-old house with four bedrooms in a small village. It meant that my children had to share bedrooms again but at that time we all had to make sacrifices. The house was in a poor condition but had some original features and we decided to renovate it. It was the second house I had been after and having been charged a considerable fee for a full survey for the first house Stephen and I had decided, foolishly, to only have a general survey done. Unfortunately, as soon as we started the renovations we realized that we had taken on a massive task. There was rot on the inside of the roof, a lot of damp and, most serious of all, we needed a new septic tank. At the time we didn't get too worried because Stephen was earning a considerable amount in the financial sector. In addition we felt confident that our improvements, which came to about £40,000, would be reflected in the price when we eventually sold the property.

Paul and Rebecca blossomed at their new school. Paul sat next to a boy called Ahmed, who became a close friend. He said that although he had been out of Tadford for many years, it was only when he started having fun with Ahmed at weekends that he learnt how good life could be outside the Church. The trouble was he began to enjoy himself too much – he himself described it as 'going a bit nuts' and he started drinking alcohol when he was 14. I was worried that he seemed easily influenced and was enjoying the drinking culture a bit too much, which was in turn distracting him from his GCSEs. It became a huge concern, but I didn't know whether I was worrying so much because of my own teenage upbringing at Tadford, where drink was so frowned upon.

Rebecca, by contrast, improved enormously. Although she initially found the change-over difficult, when she was 12 a school pal asked if she'd like to join her and go to army cadets. She took to it immediately. The cadets had the structure she was used to at Tadford, but without the corporal punishment or control, and proved to be the best of both worlds. It gave her role models to look up to, and she found adults and children who cared about her. Most significantly she learnt how to channel her boundless energy constructively and stopped behaving badly. The experience transformed her and she went twice a week until she was 18. I felt very proud of her and how far she had come.

Chapter 13

On Trial

It was only once the children were more settled that I began to realize just how damaged I had been by my time at Tadford. I had many issues. I struggled to stand up for myself. I had low self-esteem. I remained too opinionated, although I was beginning to listen to other people's views. I was too trusting and told too much about my life to people whom I hardly knew. I couldn't cope with confrontation with those I loved and was far too sensitive to what was said to me.

Making decisions was still a problem and I either made them impulsively or asked so many people for their view I couldn't remember what I had to decide. In addition, I couldn't cope if an organization, like my university, gave me instructions. I felt they were trying to control me and that had too many echoes of Tadford.

The more I thought about it the more I wanted to prove there was something seriously wrong with a Church that seemed to have the objective of crushing the individuality and spirit of its congregants, instil mortal fear into their souls and extract large sums of money from them. The only effective way of doing so was to get some sort of legal acknowledgement. It was a sad and difficult point to reach, but I felt a powerful moral responsibility to expose the Church to the general public.

I talked to Wendy, who suggested that I could sue Black, Peter and five other Church trustees for undue influence and brainwashing. I could also assert that they stopped me from continuing my education after my O Levels and even arranged my marriage to Peter.

She began working on a compensation claim based on how much I had paid out as donations and tithes, plus my many years of unpaid work in the nursery school, the Church shop and editing CDs. Wendy then set out to prove that I handed money over while I was in this brainwashed state and subjected to undue influence. The case would encapsulate everything I had believed and suffered from while I was in the Church and be the accumulation of so much that had destroyed my life. Inevitably, analysing my time there in such forensic detail was a very emotional and difficult experience, particularly as I was still struggling to cope in the world outside the Church, but I pressed on, with Wendy's backing, because I knew it was the right thing to do. The claim gradually took shape over many months, until finally it was ready.

The essence of the claim was that Black, through the means of his dominating character and apparent spirituality, as well as the support of other senior Church leaders, had exerted an overbearing influence over members of Tadford Church. The methods that the Church used to ensure the unbending obedience of its members included corporal punishment for the most minor offences, a severing of relationships with those who were not members of the Church – particularly family members – and the public ridiculing of any person who maintained independence of thought, with such people often being accused of sexual deviance or drug addiction. The Church also attempted to cut its members off from ordinary life by asserting that the outside world was defiled, and forbade the watching of TV or films and the reading of non-Christian books, as well as insisting on church attendance three or four times a week. All of these methods were underpinned by the notion that Black was directly inspired by God and that any disagreement with him – or his staff – was equivalent to a rebellion against God. Indeed, Black was shown to have given examples in his sermons of people falling ill and in some cases dying as a direct result of opposing his teachings.

The claim listed the ways in which I had been intimidated and threatened during my time at the Church, and stressed that this process had begun when I was separated from my parents at a very early age. It included detailed accounts of Black's attempt to control my wedding arrangements, of how my parents were over-ruled about my post-O-Level studies and how I was advised to be sterilized. The claim described how Black had made serious but wholly unfounded allegations about both me and my parents, and how he had insisted that Peter and I send our children to Tadford School despite there being other perfectly adequate schools in the area. That we did so meant that we were tied even more firmly to the Church and that our children were indoctrinated by the Tadford dogma. The claim outlined the amount of money Peter and I had paid out for the children's schooling and in tithes, plus the value of my work for various aspects of the Church. It also stated that my work on the CDs was largely for the promotion of Black.

I claimed half the sum Peter and I had handed over, plus what my various jobs would have been worth in the general market. I also claimed a small amount in damages.

It was going to be a test case of David and Goliath proportions. The Church was worth millions. I had very little. The trustees were a united band and could be very intimidating. I was still struggling with simple decisions and my confidence ebbed far too easily.

The case was immensely complicated. The writs were served in February against the trustees and included Black, Hugh Porter and Peter. It then took Wendy two years to prepare the case, not least because she had to travel all over the country to collect statements from former Tadford members and others who had been in contact with Black. Some individuals were too scared to talk, even though they had broken away years ago. Others felt too psychologically damaged to cope. Clive, who had been my support and guide before and after I left the Church, gave a defining statement in which he said that in his professional view: 'Those who attempt to criticize Ian Black or his Church can always expect malicious falsehoods and rumours to be aimed at them in return. Whether done publicly or "off the record", Black and his representatives will always seek to harm those whom they perceive as harming them.'

I also had to do a witness statement, itemizing everything about myself before and during my time at Tadford. I found it an emotional and difficult experience, as everything was still raw and talking about it in detail tore at my wounds. Three months after serving proceedings in court, my case was booked for a two-day pre-trial hearing in June. I attended with Stephen; Hugh Porter was present but not Black. The defendants didn't want it to go ahead. Their argument was that the case wasn't in the public interest and that there was not enough evidence to proceed. A month after the hearing the judge ruled that there was sufficient evidence to go to trial but that as neither Peter nor Black was an actual trustee of the Church, their names must be struck from the list of those I was suing. He did say that Black would instead be called up to give evidence and be cross-examined when the case was heard.

I felt enormously relieved that there would be a full trial in the public domain. I wanted people to know about the abusive way they treated children and how I had been manipulated, and for Black to stand in the dock and be accountable for his behaviour. However, nine months before the trial was due to be heard, I discovered I was pregnant. I was also in the final year of my social-work degree, so the timing could not have been worse. I was terribly shocked by the discovery, but I didn't for a moment consider having an abortion, as it was completely against my religious beliefs.

The baby was due the following May, the same month as my case against Tadford was scheduled to be heard in court. Question after question flooded my brain, from how would Peter react if he found out about my pregnancy, to how would I even manage to get to court, let alone be in a sufficiently good physical or psychological state to give evidence? I decided it was very important that Peter and any other defendant didn't get to hear about my pregnancy as I didn't want it to affect any aspect of the case.

My case was funded by legal aid and a public funding certificate was granted. My lawyer Wendy then put in a Part 36 offer, which is a widely used way of settling disputes out of court and avoids the huge expense of a trial. It can be made by either the Claimant or the Defendant. After the offer Tadford made representations to the Legal Services Commission, which led to the public funding certificate being briefly suspended shortly before the trial. It was reinstated after our appeal before the Funding Review Committee and almost immediately afterwards the case was settled. Wendy believes that when Tadford realized they had no alternative but to accept the offer or proceed to trial, they decided to accept it.

I heard the news a month before the trial was due to start. Stephen and I had just arrived at a service station off the M6 where I had arranged for Peter to pick up the children at McDonald's, as he and his aunt and uncle had planned to take them to Alton Towers. I had left the children with Stephen and was trying to keep out of sight because I didn't want Peter to see how pregnant I was. Suddenly my mobile rang and Wendy told me everything was sorted. I couldn't believe my victory and once the children had gone I treated myself to a sip from a quickly purchased bottle of champagne to celebrate. I spent much of that afternoon being driven around the countryside by Stephen, and I felt joyous, even though I didn't get my day in court. It proved to me that I could cope on my own and that I had been telling the truth.

Black had made an appeal to his congregation for funds to fight the court case. I was told it raised a staggering amount, way beyond what he needed and I have no idea what was done with the surplus. Nor am I entirely clear how the result of the case was presented to the Church members. Some members recall Black telling them that Tadford had won the case, at which point most of the congregation clapped and cheered. Black then added that, despite this, the Church was paying some of my legal fees as it would not be Christian to leave me financially disadvantaged. He reassured them that the money would go straight to the court and I would not benefit in any way. Apparently, some members believed him without question. Others thought it seemed odd because they knew people only settle out of court when they don't want to admit liability but know they are going to lose. Despite this, they didn't dare challenge Black.

Others members recall Black merely announcing that Tadford had won the case, then, after an assembly, asking one of the Church trustees to make a short statement.

* * *

None of that spoilt what was a brilliant day for me, and I couldn't wait for the children to come back and celebrate with Stephen and me. After they'd been dropped off at the service station – once again I hid out of sight – I told them my news but they were really too young to understand the implications and, like children everywhere, were much keener to tell me about their exciting day out. This was only the second time since they had left Tadford that they had seen Celia and Patrick, and they'd had a great time. Rebecca was beaming and I knew it had gone particularly well. She told me what a good time she'd had and wanted to call her father straight away to chat. But within seconds of her call I heard her joyful voice completely change. The call was short and when she put the phone down I immediately asked her what was wrong. She told me that Peter had stopped her speaking to say he didn't love her and didn't want to see her again. I was so shocked I called him immediately. He told me that as he could no longer influence the children's lives there was no point in seeing them.

That was it. There was no more contact. As the days became weeks and months I couldn't help wondering if it was pure coincidence that he had brutally cut the children out of his life on the same day that I had won my case against Tadford or whether he had been encouraged to take such drastic action to punish me. Poor Rebecca was utterly devastated. She had always been a daddy's girl and was the most affected by Peter's decision not to leave the Church and come with us. This may have been the reason why she clung on to religion for so long. His total rejection following straight after they'd had such a lovely day together was a bitter blow and affected her so much that, unbeknown to me, when children at school asked about her father she told them he was dead. She hated telling a lie but she wanted to stop their questions and to protect herself from the pain of rejection.

Her strategy didn't work. Not one day went by without her thinking about him. She missed him so badly that she texted him many times with the words, 'Pleas cm and c me.' At first he didn't reply, but eventually he sent a formal text along the lines that it wasn't in anyone's best interest for them to have a relationship, let alone meet. She still didn't want to give up and sometimes plucked up courage to ring him. She'd try to be upbeat and positive, even though she was trembling inside, as I well knew. She'd say, 'Hi, Dad. It's Becky,' and he would reply, 'Who is Becky?'

She said it was like talking to a robot and after a few months she couldn't stand it and stopped all communication. Then she began to fear that she would never see him again and that if he died none of us would know about it. It made her angry with the world, and unhappy and depressed with herself. Not surprisingly her confidence and self-esteem, boosted by her recent therapy, plummeted.

I tried to smooth things over and say her father didn't mean what he said, that he still loved her and the boys, but that in my view his behaviour was a result of his being brainwashed. I encouraged her and the three boys to keep a picture of him by their bed and bought her a circular silver frame so it would look nice. Naturally, with all that had happened to her since we left Tadford, I grew very concerned about Rebecca's well-being. She had taken the rejection very personally and felt there was a massive vacuum in her life.

Paul was furious and upset with Peter for dropping them and said he couldn't understand how a father could stop seeing his own children. He was also very upset for Rebecca and thought that Peter had been unnecessarily cruel to her. He hated seeing her cry day after day and worried that she was not sleeping well. He grew so angry that, without my knowing, he sent Peter a nasty text telling him he couldn't believe what he had done to Rebecca and making a rude comment about Black. It pleased us all immensely, but Paul in particular, when Rebecca suddenly stopped moping and, for reasons no one grasped at the time, seemed to adopt a much more positive attitude towards life.

By now I was enormously pregnant and slow-moving, but I had no chance to take things easy. Instead I was increasingly affected by stress and in May, when I was thirty-five weeks' pregnant, I started going into labour. I was rushed into hospital for an emergency Caesarean. When Naomi was born she weighed 5 lb 7 oz. Although I hadn't wanted more children, once Naomi was born I loved her totally, thought she was beautiful and believed I had been given a second chance as a mother. I felt very guilty that Paul, Rebecca, Luke and Daniel had had such difficult lives, and I wanted to bring Naomi up differently. I vowed that her life would be less structured and I would never smack her.

The first few months after the birth passed in a total blur and I seemed to be feeding Naomi all day and night. Luckily the other four adored her and tried to help when they were not at school. As the fog of having a newborn cleared a little I began sharing long telephone conversations with my sister Kerry in Canada. She was going through a bad time and feeling depressed. I was quite worried about her, particularly after she rang to say she had decided to become a Christian and had joined a church. She was the last of the family to be baptized and I feared that – despite all that she knew about cults – the church she had joined might be like Tadford.

She sounded so low that I decided to go to Canada to try to cheer her up and check on her church. I travelled over with Naomi and luckily Rebecca's headmaster gave her permission to miss school so she could come too. I left the three boys at home with Stephen, but felt very anxious about whether they would be OK.

Kerry and I had wonderful talks and bonded in a way we never had done before. I also got to know her children, Carla and Inigo, much better than I had done previously. I was as supportive as I could be and she thanked me for being level-headed and helping her to work things through. I also saw her church and was reassured that everyone was genuinely encouraged to have their own thoughts and beliefs.

I loved Canada and the outdoor lifestyle, and one day Kerry's husband, Neil, said it was a fantastic place to bring up children and suggested that we all come out to live there and make a fresh start. I was quite worried about Paul's drinking and thought moving us all to Canada might get him away from any bad influences.

When I returned home I discussed the idea with Stephen, who said he thoroughly approved. It was very exciting and we decided to get married first, then sell the house and finally emigrate. We planned that I'd get a student visa so I could go back to social work, while Stephen could set up some sort of business in Canada. Paul, Rebecca, Luke and Daniel all said they were happy to come too, provided that if it went wrong we come back to England to live. Paul had just finished his GCSEs, although he had not done very well, and

Rebecca was about to start her GCSE syllabus. So it seemed a case of either going quickly or waiting two years. We decided on the former and set the wheels in motion. We had a quiet wedding early the following year, put the house up for sale and then, just as we hoped our plans would really take off, everything started to go incredibly wrong. I discovered to my enormous shock that there was a land dispute hanging over my house. It concerned a tiny piece of land that controlled the drainage of the septic tank and would undoubtedly affect any future sale. I hadn't been told about it when I bought the house, but it meant it would be virtually impossible to sell until it was sorted out.

I wanted to wait until the dispute was resolved and the house was sold before we emigrated, but Stephen was keen to go as soon as possible. He was so insistent about it that, partly because of my inability to stand my ground and partly because I was so busy with Naomi, I didn't have the strength or mental capacity to argue with him. In the end we were around longer than we thought as it took us nearly a year to get organized. During that time we had various potential house purchasers but each one backed down once the land dispute was revealed.

When we finally arrived in Canada the following January a series of disasters unfolded right from the moment we landed. The student visa I was given allowed only twenty hours' work a week. Not only that, but I also discovered my social-work course didn't start until March. In addition, arriving with a student visa meant we had to pay school fees for the four older children. This was a huge financial commitment, especially as we still hadn't sold the house in England. The only good thing was that we rented a 1970s red-brick house only a few miles away from Kerry and so could see a lot of each other. We all loved the outdoor life, but we were haemorrhaging money, not least because so many of our expenses had to be multiplied seven times. It took me until March to sort out the paperwork and start on my course. Stephen, however, was unable to find any work, and sank into a depression. It all meant that I couldn't rely on him financially or emotionally.

Eventually, in May, we managed to sell the house, for a fraction of what it was worth, and the capital was far too small to pay off our debts. Things went from bad to worse and culminated in Luke becoming desperately ill with appendicitis. He hadn't been feeling well for a few days, then one evening he was suddenly in so much pain that he found it difficult to move and started vomiting. I rushed him to the doctor, who told me to take him to hospital, and he was operated on almost immediately as there was fear of rupture. They successfully removed his appendix and poor Luke made a slow but steady recovery.

I was extremely relieved that he was on the mend, but the cost of his treatment made severe inroads into our depleted finances. We decided that our only option was to come home and we returned back to England that June.

I had lost all my money, but my supportive Paul, who had happily cut right down on his drinking while we were away, continued to be positive, caring and sanguine. He told me that even if our trip to Canada had failed it had been a cool idea to try. I hugged him tight and cried.

Chapter 14

A Family Reunited

We arrived back penniless and with huge debts. I had promised the children that if we ever returned we would settle near our old house where all their friends were, but Stephen insisted that a city thirty miles away would provide better job opportunities and I felt too beaten by our catastrophic trip to fight him. I managed to find a house to rent that the local council agreed to pay for and he got a job as an underwriter at a stockbrokers.

Our marriage was effectively over but we limped on for a little longer because I didn't have the strength to deal with any more upheaval, and couldn't face the prospect of my darling children living through another broken relationship.

Luckily four out of five of the children stayed in good shape. Paul started a diploma in engineering at the local technical college and Rebecca went to sixth-form college to do A Levels in sociology, history and Chinese.

Naomi went to a heavily subsidized nursery attached to a church school and Daniel went to secondary school. It was just Luke who was really struggling. I got him into the same school as Daniel because, like many twins, they were basically inseparable, but he didn't settle, refused to attend, and it became almost impossible to get him out of bed in the morning. At first I thought he was just being difficult but I gradually realized he wasn't at all well. He hadn't properly recovered from the operation and the desperate situation in Canada, and was so exhausted that, if I let him, he would sleep all day. I took him to the doctor, who diagnosed depression but wouldn't give him any medication. He was also having problems with food and didn't want to eat. To make matters worse, he was at constant loggerheads with Stephen, although none of us understood quite why.

Weeks went by and he didn't improve, and I spent more time supporting him than the other four put together. I felt he was suffering from the accumulation of everything that had happened to him, including his heart murmur, his bedwetting, being beaten as a child, his dislike of Stephen and the general turmoil in his life. His attendance at school continued to worsen, and when it dropped to about 80 per cent the education authorities got involved. Every other day someone would either phone me or come round to the house to check up on him, and after a while I was threatened that I would be taken to court for not sending him to school.

Stephen and I struggled through Christmas but we were so broke that I couldn't even afford to give the children presents and went to a supermarket late on Christmas Eve to get a half-price turkey. I finally told Stephen he had to leave and in the New Year I became a single mother of five. I lived on £80 a fortnight from income support plus Peter's maintenance, which had dropped considerably as we had now been divorced for five years. Stephen, who had been made redundant, couldn't afford to pay any maintenance for Naomi.

I couldn't believe what had happened to me. I had worked so hard to start again, build up my life, protect my children and find a career, and now not only was I back to square one but I barely had enough money to feed and clothe us all. I managed to get vouchers for school uniforms for the older four children from the council. I stopped wearing make-up apart from the cheapest lipstick and didn't buy anything new to wear. Instead, I rooted round charity shops or cut-price outlets to clothe myself and the children. Children's shoes were the most difficult item to find, especially as their feet seemed to grow particularly fast during this nightmare time.

I worked out a strict food budget and counted every penny. I then went to the cheapest supermarket I could find and bought the basics just before the shop closed at the end of the day, to take advantage of any reductions and special offers. I have always valued a healthy diet, so I bought things like minced meat, pasta and raw vegetables. There was absolutely no money for yummy treats like crisps, biscuits or fizzy drinks, so ironically our impoverished diet was very healthy for us all.

I managed to get a part-time job as a social worker with the local mental-health team, timed to fit in with the hours that Naomi was at nursery. My social life was confined to our local church, which was within walking distance of where we lived. Naomi came with me but the other children, including Rebecca, didn't want to know. The members were very friendly and I told a couple of women fellow worshippers that I was going through a tough time. Without my asking they began to drop off tins of food at my home when they went on a weekly bread run to the local poor and needy. It was difficult for me to accept their generosity because I felt so ashamed and was sure there were other people who were far worse off than me. But the truth was that it was a life-saver and helped keep us going.

Meanwhile my financial situation was getting out of control. My debts had reached astronomic levels, largely because I had no means of paying off the debt on the renovation of the house I'd bought with Stephen. I just couldn't make ends meet and in the end I felt there was no alternative but to be made bankrupt. I was so ashamed and felt that I had done something terrible. I had never once got into arrears with the mortgage in all my life but now I felt like a leper. Going bankrupt meant I could no longer use credit cards or have a bank or building-society account. I had to live on cash, which was very difficult with five children as I had to make sure I had enough money for every eventuality before we went anywhere.

Shortly afterwards Dad rang to say Mum had had a fall and, as she didn't seem quite right, he was going to take her to the local hospital for a check-up. He rang back hours later to say the doctors had diagnosed a mini-stroke. It was a terrible shock, but luckily it proved to be not too serious. It did, though, make me think hard about their mortality. I loved my parents enormously and I wanted to spend as much time as I could with them, not least to try to make up for the lost years when I'd been at Tadford.

I felt a huge pull to return to where my parents lived and that summer I decided to go back for good. It wasn't going to be easy. Although Paul was now at university doing a degree in engineering, Rebecca was only half-way through her A Levels and I didn't want to disrupt her. She and I had a long talk and she said she was happy for me to go but she would stay put. I then approached the Church to ask if there were any members who wanted to let out a room. A young married couple volunteered. We all met and Rebecca and I both felt very comfortable with them. So she moved in and I paid for her rent and food. It broke my heart to leave her behind but we spoke on the phone every day and in retrospect it was a really good stepping stone for her as she had independence with security.

I rented a house that I saw advertised on the internet. It was large enough for when Paul and Rebecca came to stay, and had a good local school. We now lived very close to Mum and Dad, which we all loved. It also meant I could give them support and they could be close to their grandchildren – something they had really missed out on before.

Luke was still a dreadful worry for me, and for his grandparents, who were now able to see first-hand what I had previously only hesitantly told them on the phone. All he wanted to do was sleep and some days he barely had the strength to walk to the toilet. I took him back to the doctor and after a thorough examination he was finally diagnosed with glandular fever. He was now at an age when teenage boys are usually out enjoying themselves, but Luke had little energy for either school or a social life. It made him feel useless and he was very tearful. Fortunately the nearby hospital had a good education department for children who were outpatients and sent teachers to coach him at home. It worked well, but unfortunately they felt he was too far behind in his GCSE studies to continue where he had left off and should start again. No one told us that he could continue to follow the same GCSE curriculum and use the same examining board he had had when we had moved with Stephen, so instead he started his GCSEs all over again with a different board. It meant that, just as everyone else in his age group was finishing their GCSEs, he was starting again. Although he is a bright boy, in the end he managed only two GCSEs, in economics and graphic design, which didn't reflect his ability or help his confidence.

Money remained a huge problem and as a short-term measure I worked as a cleaner for a friend for a few weeks. Once I felt more settled I applied for a full-time job with the same mental-health team that I'd had the part-time job with, and they gave me a six-month contract. I loved the work and felt I was good at it, which gave me confidence. So much so that when the contract ended I decided to try to go back to university to gain a post-graduate qualification. I rang my old university and asked for a place. They interviewed me twice and finally offered to take me. I felt enormous relief that I could get on with my life again.

Almost a year after I went bankrupt, however, my life was suddenly thrown into turmoil once more. It began when a former member of Tadford phoned me and asked, 'Haven't you heard?'

'What?' I replied.

'Ian Black has resigned and left the Church.'

Black had apparently been involved in financial irregularities regarding the tithes he received from Church members. The trustees called a meeting and Black arrived looking thoroughly dishevelled, as if he had not slept for days. Standing in front of the assembled throng, his trembling hand holding a prepared statement, he said the following words in a deep and barely audible growl:

'I stand before you all today as a sinner, a fallen man. You have trusted me with the supreme duty of leading you, my flock, and I have failed in this task. I will not dwell upon the nature of what I have done, because I know that you are all aware of what it is that constitutes my sin but I will say that I am like the thief on the cross, unworthy before the sight of Jesus. I apologize to each and every one of you, and ask that in the fullness of time you find within your hearts the compassion and magnanimity to forgive me. I have resigned from the Church and wish that you and all who worship in this great building find a leader who is worthy of you and the tradition that has been created here.'

By the time he finished his speech everyone was shouting and screaming, and the impromptu meeting ended in complete disarray. Black had controlled the Church with two iron fists for so many years that its members were shocked and astonished by this appalling revelation. Many felt utterly betrayed and, as he strode out of the building, several angry members confronted him and gave vent to their feelings.

I couldn't believe Black had gone and when I put the phone down I burst into tears and sank to the kitchen floor. I didn't think in my wildest dreams that something like this would happen but the effect on me was almost instantaneous. Since I had left the Church, not a day had passed without my feeling that my punishment for doing so was that I might drop dead at any time. The possibility of this happening was always at the back of my mind and I frequently suffered from waves of acute anxiety. But after the phone call the feeling vanished completely and has not returned.

When the news began to sink in, I hoped that this revelation about Black would show people what he was really like and break the control he had over the members of the Church, and that they would no longer be afraid of him. I also realized it meant there was a chance for my children to see their father again. I wondered whether Peter would ring immediately and arrange a meeting, but that didn't happen.

When I got my breath back I rang the children to tell them what had happened. Paul and Rebecca were both very matter-of-fact about it. Although Paul said, 'That's amazing', there was no emotion in his voice. Rebecca, in her inimitably rational way, asked if there were any legal implications.

I then rang Luke and Daniel, who were both at a friend's house. They were as emotional as I was and we all cried. I felt compelled to see them, so I put Naomi in the car and drove off. We all rushed into each other's arms and burst into tears again. When we peeled ourselves away I noticed that their friend was looking really worried and must have thought something terrible had happened. I explained nothing bad had occurred. Quite the contrary, it was potentially good news as they would almost certainly see their Dad again. I had always believed that Black had discouraged Peter from seeing his children once he didn't get custody but that underneath it all Peter genuinely loved them. It was a very poignant time.

When I got home I tried to contact Peter but he had moved and I didn't have any up-to-date numbers. I took a big breath, rang Tadford, and asked them to give me Black's deputy Hugh Porter's phone number as I decided I'd ask him to put me in touch with Peter. To my amazement someone at Tadford gave me what I'd asked for. I then started shaking with nerves so much that it took me a few weeks to build up the courage to call. I finally rang one Saturday night. I was expecting Hugh to be frosty towards me, but he was fine. I asked him to talk to Peter and try to persuade him to get in touch with the children, and explained that Rebecca, in particular, would like to see her father.

Shortly afterwards Peter sent Rebecca a birthday card that arrived on exactly the right day. It had a ladybird on the front and he wrote, 'I love you. You can phone me any time.' He also provided his number. It was his first contact for five years.

Rebecca was the first of the children to ring her Dad. Afterwards she said she would be pleased if he wanted to be part of her life, but because he didn't come out of Tadford with us, she wasn't going to make too much effort to see him.

Paul called next. He said he wasn't sure how to talk to his father during that initial phone call, but was the first of the children to arrange a visit. He went on his own and stayed for a weekend. He and his father went to a football match together and got on very well. Peter apparently asked Paul if he was still angry with him about what had happened. The question astonished Paul as he had never known him to talk openly about his feelings. He replied that it was now all in the past and he was fine about it. He felt sad that his father had lost his family when we left and believed he must have suffered without us all. When Paul and I spoke after the visit he said it felt really strange seeing him again after so long. In particular, he couldn't get over how physically alike they were and felt he was looking at an older version of himself.

Rebecca went the weekend after Paul and felt differently about her Dad's attempted reconciliation. She said she still resented the fact that he had put the Church before his children as it was the wrong way round and that if she ever has children she will always put them first. She said that she was able eventually to get over Peter's rejection of her in the car park that day and his continued silence when she had texted him, because, amazingly for someone her age, she was able to rationalize that he was rejecting the whole family, and not just her. If I had known that, and if Paul, in particular, had known that too, then perhaps we wouldn't have worried so much and for so long about her.

Both Luke and Daniel wanted to speak to Peter, but, although Daniel rang him and they got on fine, as they had always done, Luke understandably felt very vulnerable, perhaps because subconsciously he didn't want to risk getting into any more trouble. His anxiety over whether he should call him and, if so, when, continued for months until one day, after he'd had a huge argument with me over nothing, I said to him, 'That's it. I've had enough. We're phoning Daddy.' I dialled the number and when it rang I put the phone in his hand

and said, 'Talk to your father because that is what you need to do.' I then went out of the room so he could talk in private.

He was very emotional when he came off the phone but I could see an immediate difference in him. I asked what Dad was like and he replied, 'He was a normal person again, Mum.' He explained that it had been quite an awkward call as they didn't know what to say to each other, and Peter just asked how he was and what he was up to. But he bravely asked if he could go and see him, and Peter said of course he could.

There was a big gulf between knowing in theory that he could go and see him, and plucking up the courage to actually meet him again. The process of narrowing that gap took a long time. It was going to be a massive step for him. He had missed him so much and if it didn't work it would be horrendous. He kept putting off the meeting as he was scared that Peter wouldn't like him and they wouldn't get on. At the back of my mind I was worried that Luke was still terrified of his father. In the end he asked Paul if he would come too, to help him feel more secure.

Eventually he settled on a day in February, but as the day approached he became increasingly anxious. He knew that Dad had loved him when he was young but still could not understand why he had been beaten so often.

Apart from insisting that Paul be there, he asked if I'd stay close by too. I contacted a friend, who said I was very welcome to stay the night, and Luke felt relieved. Just before we left he panicked and tried to back out. Very unusually for me I forced him to go. I told him he just had to face it. 'You know it's what you want,' I said.

He was very anxious during the journey and when we arrived at Peter's house I came to the door with him. When Peter opened the door his face lit up and his eyes filled with tears when he saw Luke. Then he grinned from ear to ear. It was wonderful to see but so sad that he had lost all those precious years.

The visit lasted two days. I picked Luke up afterwards at a prearranged point and he looked exhausted. We talked about it as I drove him home and his feelings were inevitably mixed. He too couldn't believe how physically alike Peter and Paul were but said the two of them spent a lot of time talking about football and, as he hadn't the slightest interest in the sport, he couldn't join in and sat in silence. He admitted Peter did try to talk to him too but that it was obvious he didn't know quite what to say to someone who had so frequently beaten him. He felt upset that they didn't really bond, but added rather wistfully that Peter was 'still the nice Dad I used to know'.

A more substantial reaction occurred a day or so later when he told me he felt as if a physical weight had lifted from his shoulders and, even more significantly, that he had stopped having nightmares. These had begun after we left Tadford. Each one was slightly different in its details but all contained people coming to kill him and take away his family. We used to talk about these dreams at length and I'd try to calm him. Once he'd seen his father they instantly disappeared and have not returned.

Luke and Peter then exchanged some text messages and a few phone calls, but it was about five months before he went to stay with him again, this time with Daniel. Thankfully he said it was much easier and more relaxed the second time round, perhaps because of the relaxing presence of his twin brother, but he now feels there is a lot of work that needs to be done to build up the relationship. The good thing is that he wants to make the effort. Meanwhile he is a changed person. He used to snap at me a lot and get very depressed, but after he was reunited with Peter he became more relaxed and, as a result, far easier to be with.

It is wonderful that all the children have a relationship with their father. Every child needs their Dad in their life and someone to turn to, but I admit it is difficult for me. I don't trust Tadford and worry that the children might get sucked back into the Church. I have fought very hard to keep them safe but I also realize that at some point I will not be able to protect them any longer and hope they have seen enough to make good decisions.

I now felt able to look to the future. I started working again and began to have a social life. I had made a group of friends in the local area and occasionally joined them at a campsite that had marvellous views across the Dales. I had known some of them before I went to Canada and felt close to them. There was a bar at the site but as I couldn't afford to drink I would get water with a slice of lemon so it looked like gin and tonic.

On one occasion a young man called Max, whom I'd never met before, was there. He introduced himself to me as a teacher, we started chatting and gradually developed a great friendship. We found we shared the same values and had lots in common. Initially, I was scared to get involved in another relationship as I didn't trust my own judgement, and didn't want to get hurt. I also needed to concentrate on the children and didn't want to be distracted, but Max made me feel so at ease that it hasn't been a problem. I didn't introduce him to the children until I'd known him for about six months as I didn't want men coming in and out of their lives, but we have now been together for a while and are beginning to plan our future together.

Things have moved on at Tadford since I left and it's all become rather complicated. Just before I fled, Black began to focus with his usual intensity on expanding Tadford School. He wanted to build a theatre and was incandescent when his planning application was turned down by the council. He was not a man to be thwarted and in several subsequent sermons he referred to local councillors as 'dodgy men with dubious handshakes', and described the council as a 'gutter' and the people who worked for it as 'vermin'. He said his aim was 'to ensure that the children had the very best preparation for life', adding, 'the council decided, for reasons unknown to anyone, not to let the local children learn how to act, which is something they themselves should have learnt a long time ago'. In fact the council refused planning permission as the proposed building was going to be built on an area that would have had problems with drainage.

No one knows today what has become of Black. Like Lord Lucan, he has disappeared off the face of the earth but is occasionally sighted here and there, sometimes in mundane surrounding such as one of the many Charismatic churches dotted around the country, at other times in more exotic locales, such as Honolulu or the Maldives. A former Church member telephoned me a couple of years ago to say that she was sure that she had seen him shopping in the town's supermarket, but when I spoke to her more recently she said she was not certain that it really was him. Like Lucan, he definitely was a colourful character, but this colour was purely superficial. Beneath his attractive exterior lay a dark, troubled core, which, if you ever saw it – and my family and I saw it on more occasions that we would ever have liked – left you shivering, wondering whether you had come into contact with a force that was the very opposite of the one that you had at first recognized.

Chapter 15

Looking Back

When I look back at my time at Tadford Charismatic Church I still feel aggrieved. I have no doubt that one of its aims was to kill my will. It's a horrible thing to do to anyone, but especially to a young teenage girl whose whole life was stretching out before her. Nor can I see anything genuinely religious in a leader who used his position to intimidate his congregation, take advantage of the vulnerable and break up families, and who seeks to divide and rule rather than care for and conciliate.

There was nothing humble or modest about Ian Black. Instead he had a massive ego and a grandiose style that he used to control his congregation and keep them in awe of him. In retrospect I see that almost everything he did was done to perpetuate his own power and increase his status and financial standing. It was, however, subtly disguised to imply that even God himself was relieved and grateful that Ian Black had finally arrived on earth, albeit in a small church on the outskirts of a minor commuter town. It meant that the Almighty finally had someone to do His work. It was ridiculous to believe that Tadford was the only place God wanted to be and that He filtered all His wishes through a man who lacked basic kindness and mercy. Or that He used Black as a conduit for His threats to kill anyone who so much as went shopping without permission, or attended another church. But Black excelled at alternately whipping us all into a frenzy of excitement and then turning us into a giant quivering jelly of fear. Some of his subjects saw his style as charismatic. I believe it had elements of certain mind-coercion techniques to keep people subjected to his will. His bullying manner, intransigence and uncompromising need to control undoubtedly had a crippling effect on three generations of my family.

My mother was very vulnerable when she met him, largely because of my brother Roy's mental illness. She was having a hard time coping with life and her self-esteem was low. Yet Black treated her shabbily and took advantage of her weakness by implying he had all of life's answers. Then, when she became his follower, he undermined her by repeatedly telling her she was a terrible mother, and that two of her children were evil and destined to go to Hell. I was the only one who could be saved, and because of that she should forget she had me. He even stooped so low as to accuse my father, a man of the utmost integrity and morals, of molesting me. I blame Black for nearly breaking up a loving marriage of over thirty years.

I know my parents still feel guilty about leaving me at Tadford and responsible for many of the difficulties I went through once I escaped. It's obvious in retrospect that they made a mistake. We have all had to deal with the consequences of that, but I don't blame them. I understand how they got hooked on the whole religious package and were only trying to do their best for me.

My children have also been severely affected by spending their early years in such a punitive, controlling and insular environment. Because I became so fearful for their future, I escaped with them, leaving their father behind, which meant their parents' marriage broke up in the most dramatic and traumatic circumstances. Peter's priority was to remain in the Church rather than be with his family, and because Tadford positively discouraged contact with former members my children lost their close relationship with their father. They had no idea how to cope with the world outside Tadford. Three of them, at least, have suffered physical and psychological damage. None of them remains at all religious and, despite the fact that I have retained my faith, I can't say that I blame them.

Paul withdrew into himself and during his adolescence drank far too much. Rebecca was diagnosed with post-traumatic stress disorder, and was a difficult and unhappy girl. Luke had an eating disorder, was terrified of people in authority, and suffered from low self-esteem and depression. Only Daniel seems to have escaped relatively unharmed, but then perhaps he is simply good at hiding things.

Now we have been out of the Church for well over a decade some of its very few positive side-effects have surfaced. We all have strong morals and a clear idea of the difference between good and bad. We are also all polite and well-mannered. Paul sees this as a plus, and reasons that Tadford taught him the right way to behave in life, but he believes it went about it in totally the wrong way.

Rebecca is angry about her time at Tadford and thinks her legacy was to have grown up too fast. She feels she was treated very badly and has missed out on several years of her life. She resents the way Tadford blocked her from expressing her feelings and regrets that it has had a long-lasting effect. She also feels unnecessarily guilty about how badly she behaved when we first came out.

Luke, who was still very young when we left Tadford, feels he was too young to benefit positively. About Daniel, as I have said, it's hard to really know very much, but maybe one day he will come to recognize – at the very least – the effect of seeing his twin brother regularly beaten before his eyes.

All of them hated being smacked both at home and at school, and they all state they would never smack their own children. I particularly regret smacking them. I have never smacked Naomi and it is something I now consider completely unnecessary.

Rebecca thinks corporal punishment is a form of bullying and doesn't address why a child did something wrong, but is instead, as she puts it, 'just whacking them in the hope they won't do it again'. One of her jobs has been working in social services and she told me she could relate to some of the children who were beaten by their father and taken into care. It breaks my heart.

I also feel guilty about the traumatic time they have been through after we left the Church and am grateful that they have been very generous towards me. I tried to be honest throughout and always explained what was happening to us, even when it was particularly difficult, such as our time in Canada. Rebecca has said that my being open, rather than just telling them what to do, has, in turn, helped her communicate with me about anything.

Most of all, the children have said they believe that taking them out of Tadford was the right thing to do, even though as a result their parents' marriage failed and they have had to grow up largely without their father.

I have also been badly affected by my time at Tadford. I was torn away from my parents and sister at a very vulnerable age. I resent the fact that I missed out on a normal teenage life and developing as a rounded person. I would, for example, have loved to have gone to university and lived in digs, surviving on baked beans and listening to all sorts of music. Instead my development was prescribed, restricted, controlled and narrowing. It has had a long-term effect and sometimes I still don't know where I fit into society.

I totally disapprove of the way the Church was run as a business where image and material success were valued more than compassion. Nor did I like how God was presented. To the naive newcomers who walked through the church door He was sold like a commodity. He could heal you and perform a miracle, but the price was high and part of that price was total obedience. But once you joined the Church He became a God of fear. Religion shouldn't be rammed into you so you lose the courage to make even the simplest decision. I feel I was mentally coerced into believing that Black had a direct link to Jesus and as a result I was terrified of Black's dominance and power. For many years, like most of the congregation, I believed he was a man of God, who knew my innermost thoughts, and that my own spiritual salvation rested in his hands. It made questioning his inappropriate behaviour, including his strong language and sexual innuendo, impossible to voice in public and something that instead was seen as a personal idiosyncrasy rather than a huge unpleasant flaw.

Those, like me, who did question his behaviour quickly found their position within the Church untenable.

I see what happened to me as spiritual rape. Just as a woman who is raped finds it almost impossible to trust a man again, so will I never totally recover my belief in religion or trust another religious leader. Life is often very difficult for me and, although I can come across as being very confident, often inside I am shaking like a leaf.

I believed in everything Black said, and it gave Peter and me a purpose in life, but ever since my eyes were opened to what really went on within the Church, I have found it difficult to trust people both personally and professionally. I have become more cynical and question everybody's motives. Black has, of course, now been shown to be a hypocrite. His theft from the Church cannot be described as a momentary slip. Instead, he believes in one law for himself and another for others.

And yet I still have faith. I feel I have been looked after despite everything. There have been times, especially at the tough beginning of my life outside the Church, that remain special. I am very grateful that I was somehow guided to make contact with Clive and Adam. If it wasn't for their support I would never have found the strength to escape. I am also grateful that the first house the children and I lived in after we left Tadford gave us the oasis we so badly needed.

God is still part of my life but I don't have to go to church to find Him. Now my faith is individual and more spiritual, and can be as simple as a silent time to help me deal with things. I have also wondered whether God put me in Tadford for a purpose and believe that whatever people go through should be used for the better. I hope that telling my story helps families throughout the world who have a loved one in some sort of cult-like organization, even if it just gives them hope that the light will eventually be switched on and their loved one will come back to them.

In retrospect, I can see how brainwashed I was. I believe I have overcome it in most areas of life, but sometimes it surfaces in the smallest ways. I struggled, for example, to let my children watch television and, because I had been told so often that a pub was a den of iniquity, I still find it difficult to accept that Christians can go there to drink alcohol. Equally, because I spent so many years doing what I was told, I still find confrontation and saying no difficult.

I regret that we have moved home too many times, which can't have been easy for my children. I put it down to the difficulties I had in making decisions. If you don't naturally learn how to evaluate change at the right time, it is hard suddenly to master it. I found it almost impossible to foresee what might happen in the future and, as a consequence, made short-sighted decisions.

But I have always done my best for my children and I am pleased that all four of them (I'm not counting Naomi, who is too young to have been involved) have been very supportive of the book. I am also very proud of them. Paul has done well at university and has his degree in engineering. Rebecca has a marvellous job as a probation officer. Luke is recovering his strength and thoroughly enjoying his studies in graphic design, and Daniel is working to be a sports psychologist.

I am so grateful that in spite of all our traumas we have always been and remain very close. My children have always been my world and no words can adequately express how much I love them.

Afterword

The World of Cults

As my children and I found to our considerable cost, cults are one of the most insidious features of modern life, breaking up families and destroying individuals.

Most people think they could never be drawn into a cult, and that only the weak and vulnerable are at risk, the sort of people who are clearly inadequate, not very bright, and who come from a dysfunctional family and are poorly educated. My story shows that they are mistaken. The truth is that individuals rarely join a cult of their own free will. Most cult members are targeted by the cult leader and his team of supporters and, although a person's age doesn't matter, their ability to work and produce money for the cult does.

Cults are not interested in the needy or lost souls vaguely searching for something to cling on to. Nor do they target people who have no philosophical curiosity or whose life centres around such things as playing football or buying clothes. Even if they tried to lure such people in, they are unlikely to succeed as these types of people are often streetwise and not easily fooled. The ideal candidate to be drawn into a cult is intelligent, idealistic and well educated, with a good earning capacity, and intellectually or spiritually curious; someone who ponders the great questions such as: What is the meaning of life? Why are we here? What is my role on earth? What happens after death?

Although such people are not intrinsically vulnerable, they are generally more open to someone who claims to know all the answers, promises to give meaning to their life and provides them with a compelling motive for the future. They are particularly susceptible when they are at a low point in their lives or are going through a time of significant change. Most at risk are young people leaving home and going to university, those who have lost someone close to them through ill-health or an accident and older people whose children have left home.

Defining what is and is not a cult is not always easy. Some cults try to present themselves as legitimate by careful choice of language, while other dubious groups may be legitimate but display cult-like characteristics. My experience with Tadford Charismatic Church reveals a number of cult-like techniques that were used on me and my family. These can be seen in the manner I was brought into the Church, what happened to me when I was in it and my experiences once I escaped.

According to Ian Haworth at the Cult Information Centre, a cult has all of the following characteristics:

- It uses psychological coercion to recruit, indoctrinate and retain its members.
- It forms an elitist, totalitarian society.
- Its founder-leader is self-appointed, dogmatic, messianic, not accountable and charismatic.
- It believes the end justifies the means in order to solicit funds or recruit people.
- Its wealth does not benefit its members or society.

Some groups have only some of the above characteristics and, while they cannot be strictly classified as a cult, they do still prey on members' sensibilities.

Once a potential individual is targeted there are several ways in which a cult tries to recruit him or her. Rather than explain what the group believes or what its programme consists of, it will insist that words are not enough and that the individual needs to come to a group meeting to understand properly what the organization is about. If the individual agrees when they arrive they will find that everyone seems welcoming, friendly and enthusiastic. This is no coincidence. Members are told to appear as if they are happy in order to encourage newcomers to commit, and they know from experience that they will be reprimanded if they are not.

The targets are also programmed to give them the impression that the only way to feel comfortable is to join the group. After the first meeting a committed cult member will keep in close contact with the newcomer and call repeatedly, often showing enormous concern about the target's welfare, to keep up the pressure. Most cults will also tell their target that they are not a cult. This is a pre-emptive strike against the warnings from friends and family members that they know will come. The cult will also be carefully deceptive by telling the target one thing when something else is the truth, so that what they might see in the cult's shop window, as it were, is not what is on offer inside. The cult might deceive, for example by saying how it helps the poor, or supports research, or peace, or the environment, when the reality is that it does no such thing. The truth about the cult will be introduced slowly and piecemeal, so the newcomer is less likely to notice the gradual change, until eventually they are doing and believing things that at the start would have caused them to walk away.

Cults use a wide range of recognized techniques of mind control or coercion to ensure that would-be members behave according to their rules.

All of them are techniques that will damage people emotionally, spiritually, financially and sometimes even physically. These usually include:

Hypnosis: This is often thinly disguised as relaxation or meditation.

Peer-group pressure: Few people want to be the odd one out in a group situation and would much prefer to belong.

Love bombing: It is common within cults to create a sense of family and friendship by hugging, kissing, touching and flattering a newcomer, in the hope that they feel they have made instant new friends.

Rejection of old values: A person's former values and beliefs will be constantly denounced as a way to speed up the acceptance of a new lifestyle.

Confusing doctrine: Members have to endure long, deliberately incomprehensible lectures to programme them to accept what they hear without question.

Non-verbal communication: Subliminal messages are implanted in these lectures by stressing certain key words or phrases.

Sleep deprivation and fatigue: Members can be kept so busy with compulsory meetings and activities that they don't have enough rest or sleep, and become too tired to think about their involvement and what it means. In addition, members do not have any privacy for private contemplation. This reduces their ability to logically evaluate what they hear or to understand what is happening to them, leading to feelings of vulnerability and disorientation.

Dress codes: Insistence on a group dress code removes a person's sense of individuality and style.

Chanting and singing: Insistence on endless group repetition of certain chants and phrases helps eliminate non-cult ideas and thoughts.

Ethical double standards: Members are urged to be obedient to the cult and to follow cult rules meticulously. They are also encouraged to be self-revealing and open in the group and confess all to the leaders. However, outside the group they are encouraged to act unethically and try to manipulate non-members to join the cult, either by deceiving them or revealing very little about themselves or the group. A cult tries to build on guilt by creating an us-and-them mentality. The more afraid of the outside world the members become, the more likely they will be to stay within the cult.

Confession: Members are kept under pressure not to keep any secrets from the group and private thoughts are discouraged. Instead, everyone is urged to watch out for other members of the cult who might be 'struggling' and report what they see to a senior member. Information given in deepest confidence is automatically reported. Members will also be encouraged to confess personal weaknesses, wrongdoing and any feelings of doubt to the leader, which in turn destroys their ego and sense of worth. As a result, cult members often try to hide their true thoughts and feelings, and instead behave in a way that, on the surface at least, makes them appear to be an ideal cult member.

In other words, members are encouraged not only to deceive outsiders and fellow cult members, but also themselves. It means that cult friendships are almost always superficial. Close friendships rarely exist because members are too scared to reveal their true feelings. This suits the leaders of the cult, who, in seeing firm friendships as a threat to their own power, will try to destroy them.

Guilt: Cults try to instil a feeling of guilt by exaggerating what they call 'sins' in a former lifestyle to encourage an individual's need for 'salvation' within the group.

Financial commitment: Members are encouraged to 'burn bridges to their past' by handing over financial assets or making large donations. In reality, it traps them or at the very least makes them very dependent on the group.

Finger-pointing: Pointing to the shortcomings of the outside world and other cults creates a false sense of righteousness within the group.

Flaunting the power of the cult: The cult will make extravagant promises, which will often include power and salvation to all its members. It is a method of promotion, ensuring that the cult will remain accepted by its members.

Isolation: The cult actively encourages newcomers to break contact with family and friends and not to see them. Not only does this physical isolation lead to loneliness, it also induces a loss of reality.

Replacement of relationships: Cults arrange marriages and 'families' among its members to destroy pre-cult families.

Controlled approval: Similar actions are alternately rewarded and punished, which makes individuals feel vulnerable, confused and disorientated.

Change of diet: Insisting on special diets and/or fasting makes members feel disorientated and susceptible to emotional outbursts.

Questions: Many cults do not allow questions or open discussion about themselves. Members are told not to read any general information that comes from outside the cult. This will be described as 'evil' or 'spiritual pornography', especially when it is critical of the cult. Instead, members are told that only information supplied by the cult is true. Some cults will go to the extreme of expelling a member from the group if he or she is caught breaking this rule. This encourages members to automatically accept what the cult promotes.

Fear: Cults thrive on their members' fear that they will go to Hell if they don't do and think as the cult tells them. As a result, even the slightest 'negative' thought, word or action of a member is exaggerated out of all proportion by cult leaders. Individuals are therefore likely to remain loyal and obedient to the group.

In general the cult exerts a totalitarian control over how its members live, encompassing what they should read, think and eat, and how they should dress and spend their leisure time.

Many people believe that people who join religious groups have only themselves to blame. Ian Haworth, the General Secretary of Cult Information Centre, believes that cult members are victims and need help. Instead, they are often treated with hostility after they have left the cult.

It is difficult to understand just how manipulative a group can be. Another misconception is that it can take weeks, if not months, for a person's mind to be controlled. Graham Baldwin of Catalyst, another charitable organization that provides support, believes this can be achieved in as little as three or four days. He says:

'The mind-control techniques used against an unsuspecting individual breaks the person down physically and mentally and removes their ability to think freely and critically for themselves.

'At the end of the three- or four-day period he or she is likely to go through a profound personality change. Not only will the individual have lost the ability to criticize the cult, but they will also behave in the way the cult wants even though it may go against their former moral code, whether it derived from a religious belief, their family or even the law of the land.'

One essential characteristic of a cult is that it has a single charismatic leader. This individual will need to be the centre of attention, have a strong personality, and be motivated by power and money. Some leaders are downright greedy and seek as much wealth as possible, often through generous donations from their followers. Above all, a leader will be seen as the supreme authority. He may delegate certain power to a few carefully chosen subordinates, but only those whom he knows will totally abide by his wishes. There is no appeal against his decisions. His word is final.

The leader will inevitably have a large ego, which can lead to delusions of grandeur. He will believe he is a prophet and God's representative on earth, and that he has a unique ability to communicate directly with God. It is a useful way of encouraging members to believe that disagreeing with their leader is equivalent to disagreeing with God. The premise they work on is that if you can make a person behave the way you want, you can make that person believe the way you want.

Cult members are taught not to question the teachings, practices or ideas of the leader. This enables the leader to encourage members to have an unhealthy dependence on him, which works to the detriment of the member, whether it is financially, psychologically, financially or socially. The leader's lust for power can also be used to exploit members of the cult sexually.

Graham Baldwin has been a counsellor for twenty-five years and specializes in working with families or individuals who have been involved with religious groups. He believes that cults are not about what a person believes but about how they are controlled and manipulated. 'In order to retain power the cult leader has to destroy the ego of those around him,' he says. 'It is the first and most manipulative form of control and it ensures continuous dependence on the leader. The usual pattern is that newcomers will be encouraged to hand the responsibility for themselves over to their leader, initially enthusiastically, then through fear. Individuals don't give up the right to make a decision. They stop making decisions because they no longer believe they are capable of making any.'

Cults are mostly a post-war phenomenon and are largely divided into two types: 'religious' cults and 'therapy' cults. Religious cults became common in the sixties. World religions in themselves are not cults, but cults are often based around them. They use a pre-established belief system as their base, but it is mind-control techniques, not the belief system, that qualifies them to be singled out as a cult.

A cult leader will state a member can only be 'saved' in his Church and that other Churches don't know what they are talking about. What's more, if the individual leaves, he will surely be on the road to Hell. The leader

gives the impression that not only are his members God's storm-troopers but they also have the ability to change the world. This is part of the technique to keep people in the group and support it without thinking about whether what it does is right or wrong. If this contrived philosophy makes them afraid of the outside world, so much the better. It is also a way for the leader to flex his power. Cult leaders expect and want to be feared.

Since the seventies there has been a rise in therapy, self-improvement and healing cults. These cults tend to canvass members by offering intensive courses, often over a long weekend, claiming to assist people to a different and better life. Both religious and therapy cults are increasing in number, but exact statistics are difficult to come by as most groups are secretive and are usually only discovered when someone complains about them.

Families can be devastated when a family member joins a cult. For every person who is recruited into a cult there are usually at least three others who grieve for them. It can be agony to try to communicate with someone who turns into a stranger once they have joined a group. Many parents who have lost a child to a cult compare the experience to a living death. Some claim it is even harder to cope with than an actual death as there is nothing final and no end to the pain, grief and heartache.

Because the mind of a cult member is manipulated and altered it is usually impossible to have a rational conversation with them about where they are and what they are doing. You can talk to them until you are blue in the face to try to get them to think logically and rationally, but this is only possible once they can see the situation they are in more objectively. Fortunately, it can happen. Sometimes the realization that they are in a cult comes slowly and a member will start to break the rules and ask questions. This often results in their being ostracized, which in turn leads to their asking more questions and possibly leaving. At other times it can be as instant as turning on a light switch. This can be the result of something as apparently minor as the public humiliation of a fellow member who is known to be a good person.

It is, however, recognized that it is easier to get an individual out of a cult than to get the cult out of an individual. When someone is bombarded by techniques of mind control, their mind not only becomes less flexible, it also seems to swallow up their personality. Elizabeth Tylden, the eminent family psychiatrist who died in 1999, was well known for her work with people traumatized by religious cults that use mind-control techniques. She explained that individuals come out of a cult with two personalities: the one the person went in with and the subsequent cult personality. This sets up a tug-of-war inside the person that can go on indefinitely. To prevent this, the cult personality must be eroded so that the original personality, which never completely disappears, can resurface. This activates the person's critical faculties and enables a return to normality. Tylden was convinced that, with the right help, most healing could be done in a few months and completed in about a year.

When people first leave a cult they are usually withdrawn, confused, disorientated and emotional. They can have suicidal tendencies, panic, feel guilty, be neurotic and have abnormal weight gain or loss. It is common for them to suffer from both amnesia and insomnia. They find it difficult to form intimate relationships, lose their sense of humour and have poor judgement. Decision-making is found to be particularly difficult, and this is part and parcel of the closing down of the critical mind.

An additional difficulty for ex-members is to work out who they are and what they believe in. The rules, behaviour patterns and boundaries of the world they knew were demolished in the cult, and so they need to eradicate the cult rules before they can move forward. This leads to a confused in-between period when they have no rules or guidelines of behaviour on which to rely. At some point, too, they inevitably worry that if they mentally attack the cult there will be retribution of some sort.

Graham Baldwin believes that with the right help ex-cult members are rarely permanently damaged but that about 4 per cent will have long-term psychiatric problems. Individuals need to be given help to challenge the cult rules and see them for what they are so they can understand what has happened to them. Unfortunately, there will always be some rules that lurk in the back of their mind and, unless each one is dealt with, these can haunt them for years.

One way to cope is to learn how to confront the negative. Cognitive behavioural therapy (CBT) has proved useful in this respect and helps people challenge bad ideas by questioning whether they are logical, true and helpful. The difficulty is that most people listen to commands and do things when someone in authority tells them to. Problems occur when people who are given authority over other people take their power to extremes and start down the road of abuse.

Useful Contacts

Catalyst
Thames House
65–67 Kingston Road
New Malden
Surrey
KT3 3PB
Tel: 020 8949 7877

The Churches' Child Protection Advisory Service
  (CCPAS)
PO Box 133
Swanley
Kent
BR8 7UQ
Tel: 0845 120 4550
www.ccpas.co.uk

Cult Awareness and Information Centre (CAIC)
www.culthelp.info

Cult Information Centre (CIC)
BCM Cults
London
WC1N 3XX
Tel: 0845 4500 868
www.cultinformation.org.uk

The Family Survival Trust (TFST)
BCM Box 2306
London
WC1N 3XX
Tel: 0845 603 7121
www.familysurvivaltrust.org

**FECRIS (European Federation of Centres of Research
and Information on Sectarianism)**
26A, rue Espérandieu
F-13001 Marseille
France
www.fecris.org

Call me evil, let me go

Information Network Focus on Religious Movements (INFORM)
Houghton Street
London
WC2A 2AE
UK
Tel: 020 7955 7654
www.inform.ac

International Cultic Studies Association (ICSA)
www.icsahome.com